THE PRIME OF MISS JEAN BRODIE, by Jay
Presson Allen, adapted from the novel by Muriel Spark,
directed by Michael Langham, was presented by Robert
Whitehead in association with Robert W. Dowling at the
Helen Hayes Theatre, N.Y.C.

CAST OF CHARACTERS
(*In Order of Appearance*)

SISTER HELENA	*Denise Huot*
MR. PERRY	*Douglas Watson*
JEAN BRODIE	*Zoe Caldwell*
SANDY	*Amy Taubin*
JENNY	*Diana Davila*
MONICA	*Catherine Burns*
MARY MACGREGOR	*Kathryn Baumann*
MISS MACKAY	*Lennox Milne*
GORDON LOWTHER	*Joseph Maher*
TEDDY LLOYD	*Roy Cooper*
MCCREADY	*Brooks Morton*
MISS CAMPBELL	*Sheila Coonan*

CITIZENS, GIRL GUIDES, SCHOOLGIRLS: *Roberta Maxwell,
Celia Watson, Nora Heflin, Mady Heflin, Jane Act-
man, Doreen Miller, Donna Conforti, Stephanie
Shepphard, Jami Fields, Jim Oyster, Brooks Morton,
Janice Mars, Jack Knight.*

ACT ONE

The action of the play occurs in Edinburgh, Scotland,
now, and from 1931 to 1933.

ACT TWO

The action continues from 1933 to 1936.

ACT THREE

The action continues two and a half years later.

3

PRODUCTION NOTE

This play can be staged effectively on a bare stage, with drapes or a cyclorama, and the use of area lighting. Only the minimum of props needed to establish the various scenes should be used. Since long stage waits between scenes are of course undesirable, it is suggested that the actors themselves bring on the necessary pieces of furniture: for example, a desk on rollers and the chairs for the classroom and office scenes; lockers, also on rollers, for the locker room scenes, etc. Imaginative direction along these lines can appreciably enhance the play's values.

4

The Prime of Miss Jean Brodie

A DRAMA IN THREE ACTS

By Jay Presson Allen

Adapted from the Novel

by Muriel Spark

SAMUEL FRENCH, INC.

45 WEST 25TH STREET   NEW

7623 SUNSET BOULEVARD HOLLYW

LONDON

The Prime of Miss Jean Brodie

ACT ONE

SCENE 1

MR. PERRY *sits quietly on convent bench. From behind, a* NUN *approaches silently. She stands quietly for a moment before she speaks.*

HELENA. I am Sister Helena.

(Startled, the MAN *rises, faces her.)*

MR. PERRY. Sister Helena. I'm so very glad to meet you. At last. (*Impulsively, he thrusts out his hand, then tentatively withdraws it.*) I'm afraid I don't know what's customary. Doesn't one . . . shake hands? In a convent?

HELENA. (*Blandly.*) I have no idea. This is the first time in twenty-seven years that question has come up. (*She does not take his hand, but sits instead.*)

MR. PERRY. A cloistered nunnery is pretty exotic territory to a Baptist from West Virginia.

HELENA. Total immersion?

MR. PERRY. What? Oh, yes. When I was four.

HELENA. Only four? Didn't it frighten you? Being ducked?

MR. PERRY. Yes. I bit the preacher's hand. But he just pushed me under until I choked and let go.

HELENA. And did this experience confirm you in the Baptist persuasion?

MR. PERRY. It confirmed me in the persuasion that if

5

someone holds you under water long enough, you will drown. (*A moment of silence.*) Sister Helena . . . I know that only a Papal dispensation frees you to receive visitors —journalists like myself—

HELENA. Forces. The Papal dispensation was enforced on me. Since my writing has become so surprisingly well known—

MR. PERRY. Well, when a book called *The Transfiguration of the Common Place*, written by a cloistered nun, becomes what we Americans refer to as a runaway best seller . . . it is bound to create enormous excitement. My publishers have sent me almost three thousand miles because of that excitement.

HELENA. I quite understand, Mr. Perry—I am like Balzac's dancing dog . . . it isn't the dance that's so wondrous, but that it's done by a dog. So it is with a *thinking* nun.

MR. PERRY. Thousands of readers have found your book profoundly illuminating. They are *naturally* curious, and particularly about the autobiographical implications—

HELENA. (*Coldly.*) There are *no* autobiographical implications in my book.

MR. PERRY. (*Cautiously.*) Are you serious?

HELENA. Mr. Perry, what do you think my book is about?

MR. PERRY. I think at its heart . . . it is about the destruction and reconstruction of a soul.

HELENA. (*Flatly.*) I think—at its heart—it is about the cultivation of spiritual common sense.

MR. PERRY. "That's what makes horse races."

HELENA. (*Smiles.*) I will try to answer your questions, Mr. Perry.

MR. PERRY. Thank you, Sister Helena. You grew up and were educated here in Edinburgh . . . but not as a Catholic. Were your parents strong Calvinists?

HELENA. My family held no extreme or passionate beliefs.

MR. PERRY. Was that remiss of them?

HELENA. As a child I found their—passivity—*dull*. For stimulation . . . I looked elsewhere.

MR. PERRY. To literature? Were you deeply influenced by your reading?

HELENA. I was influenced by reading *The City of God* by St. Augustine. Do you know it?

MR. PERRY. No, I'm sorry, I've never read it. But, what I actually meant was were you affected by the literature of the period?

HELENA. No, not at all.

MR. PERRY. Then perhaps you came under the influence of some particular person—a teacher, perhaps?

HELENA. A . . . teacher . . . yes, I was quite strongly influenced by a teacher.

MR. PERRY. A man?

HELENA. No. It was . . . a Miss Jean Brodie . . . a Miss Jean Brodie in her prime.

(*LIGHTS dim on convent bench, but* HELENA *and* PERRY *remain visible.*)

ACT ONE

SCENE 2

LIGHTS dim up on classroom. GIRLS *enter to their seats.* BRODIE *enters, takes position behind desk. She brings on Giotto painting which she places over portrait of Stanley Baldwin which has been preset on blackboard.*

GIRLS. Good morning, Miss Brodie.

BRODIE. Little girls. I am in the business of putting old heads on young shoulders, and all my pupils are the creme de la creme. Give me a girl at an impressionable age, and she is mine for life. You girls are my vocation. If I were to receive a proposal of marriage tomorrow from the Lord Lyon King-of-Arms, I would decline it. I am dedicated to you in my prime. And my summer in Italy has convinced me that I am *truly* in my prime. Prop up your books in case of intruders . . . if there are intruders, we are doing our history. But we will not do our history, rather I want to tell you of my summer and the man I met in the Borghese gardens and of the paintings I saw. Can anyone tell me who is the greatest Italian painter?

LITTLE GIRL. Leonardo da Vinci, Miss Brodie.

BRODIE. That is incorrect. The answer is Giotto; he is my favorite. Observe, little girls, Stanley Baldwin, who got in as Prime Minister and got out again ere long. Our headmistress, Miss Mackay, retains him on the walls because she believes in the slogan, "Safety First." But Safety does not come first. Goodness, Truth and Beauty come first. I want to tell you of a moment in my life when I was very young, though older than the man himself. His name was Hugh. I fell deeply in love with Hugh in the last year of the war, but he fell on Flanders' Field. Louise, are you thinking of doing a day's washing? You have your sleeves rolled up. I won't have to do with girls who roll up the sleeves of their blouses. Roll them down at once, we are civilized beings. He fell the week before Armistice was declared. He fell like an autumn leaf. Remind me to show you the map of Flanders and the spot where my lover was laid to sleep forever, before you were born. He was poor, but a hardworking and clever scholar. He said, when he asked me to marry him, "We shall have to drink water and walk slow." That was Hugh's country way of expressing that we would live quietly. Hugh was killed the day before Armistice was declared. "Come autumn sae pensive in yellow and grey, and soothe me wi' tiding of nature's decay." Robert Burns. Hugh fell like an autumn leaf. (MONICA *beings to sniffle.*) After the Armistice there was a general election and people were saying "Hang the Kaiser." But Hugh was one of the Flowers of the Forest, lying in his grave . . .

(MONICA *is now openly crying. The door opens to admit*

Miss Mackay, *the Headmistress. She is a brisk, no-nonsense, homely woman.*)

Mackay. Good morning, Miss Brodie, girls.

Girls. Good morning, Miss Mackay.

Mackay. (*To* Brodie, *not altogether a compliment.*) What a colorful frock.

Brodie. Color enlivens the spirit, does it not?

Mackay. Perhaps . . . (*Gives the* Girls *a look, smiles.* Miss Mackay's *smiles, however, are never without ambiguity.*) Though I sometimes wonder if the spirits of the girls *need* enlivening. (*At this juncture, a little sob escapes* Monica.) My word. What can be ailing the spirits of this little girl? (*Addresses* Monica.)

(*The only answer to this question is another, bolder sob.* Sandy *gives* Monica *vicious but unseen punch in the back.*)

Brodie. (*Calmly.*) Monica cries easily.

Mackay. Well, Monica, perhaps you would like to tell me why you are crying.

Brodie. (*Calmly.*) She is moved by a story I have been telling. The Battle of Flodden.

Mackay. (*Disapproving.*) Crying over a history lesson!

Brodie. It is a moving story. The night before Flodden at the Mercat Cross beside St. Giles, a ghostly herald was heard reading the names of all the noble families of Scotland beginning with the king. After the battle there was not one family that had not suffered grievous loss, as you well know, Miss Mackay.

Mackay. (*Briskly.*) To be sure. Well, girls, I know you're going to work hard at every subject this year. A good beginning makes a good ending. I hope you all had a splendid holiday and I look forward to your splendid essays on how you spent them. You shouldn't be crying over history at your age. My word! Good morning, Miss Brodie!

BRODIE. Good morning, Miss Mackay. (MISS MACKAY *shoots a look of distrust at* BRODIE, *then notices the Giotto, the deposed Stanley Baldwin. She hesitates, frowns, then, giving one last look of disapproval at* BRODIE, *at Giotto, at the whole* CLASS, *she exits. To* MONICA.) You did well not to answer the question put to you. It is best, when in difficulties, to say never a word, neither black nor white.

SANDY. But you did, Miss Brodie. You were in difficulty and you made up about Flodden.

BRODIE. Sandy, please try to do as I say, not as I do. Remember that you are a child, Sandy, and far from your prime. Now—as I was attempting to say—speech is silver but silence is golden. Mary MacGregor!

MARY. G— G— Golden?

BRODIE. What did I say was golden?

MARY. The fa—falling leaves?

BRODIE. Plainly, you were not listening to me. If you little girls would listen to me, I would make of you the creme de la creme! That is to say, Life's Elite! My teaching methods have been decried in some quarters as unsuitable for a conservative school like Marcia Blaine. That is to say, a school dedicated to the status quo. Can anyone define status quo? Monica? (MONICA *sobs*.) Sandy, define status quo.

SANDY. Does it mean staying the same?

BRODIE. That is correct. I can always depend on Sandy. Staying the same to the point of petrification. P.E.T.R.I.-F.I.C.A.T.I.O.N. But there needs must be a leaven in the lump. I do not intend to devote my prime to petrification. For this refusal I have been the intended victim of many plots. But the gangs who oppose me shall not succeed. If they want to get rid of me they will have to assassinate me.

GIRLS. Oh!

(*LIGHTS dim out on classroom.*)

ACT ONE

SCENE 3

LIGHTS up on HELENA *and* PERRY.

MR. PERRY. In her prime?

HELENA. Yes. She was an expert on Charlotte Bronte's love life . . . We were taught the advantages to the skin of cleansing cream and of the existence of Einstein, and that God had a near-Eastern counterpart named Allah. Miss Brodie marked us as her own, and we became famous in the school. Which is to say, were held in suspicion and not much liked.

MR. PERRY. What is the main thing about Miss Brodie you remember?

HELENA. That she was exciting. The cloisters will be free now. I am permitted to show you the gardens if that would interest you.

MR. PERRY. Oh, yes, of course. But, you were saying about this teacher, that she was exciting. In what way?

HELENA. Well, we were growing up and Miss Brodie . . . Miss Brodie's prime was very real to us . . . and very exciting.

(LIGHTS out.)

ACT ONE

SCENE 4

LIGHTS up on gallery.

BRODIE. Now, girls, in this part of the gallery I have been especially wanting to show you Boucher's famous painting of Madame de Pompadour . . .

(GIRL GUIDES *enter Up Right.*)

GIRL GUIDES. There's the Rembrandt!

JENNY. Oh, Girl Guides!

MONICA. A lot of girls at school belong to the Girl Guides!

BRODIE. For those who like that sort of thing, that is the sort of thing they like. Girls . . . voila! Madame de Pompadour!

LLOYD. (*Appears Up Center. Notices* BRODIE, *grins delightedly.*) Ah, the dangerous Miss Brodie!

BRODIE. (*Attempting to hide her excitement at this unexpected meeting with* LLOYD.) By whom, pray, am I considered dangerous?

LLOYD. It is the consensus. Your girls are said to be vastly informed on subjects irrelevant to the accepted curriculum. Most heinous of all, you are said to inculcate no team spirit. Is that true, girls? Does Miss Brodie incite you to shirk your duties on the hockey field?

BRODIE. Girls, this is Mr. Lloyd. As some of you may know, Mr. Lloyd teaches art in the Senior School. Mr. Lloyd, phrases like the "team spirit" are always employed to cut across individualism. Florence Nightingale knew nothing of the team spirit! Her mission was to save life regardless of the team to which it belonged. Cleopatra knew nothing of the team spirit if you read your Shakespeare. And where would the team spirit have got Anna Pavlova? She is the great prima ballerina, and the corps de ballet have the "team spirit."

LLOYD. Ah, Miss Brodie, you ARE dangerous!

BRODIE. Girls! It's time to go home.

MONICA. But it's so early.

BRODIE. Come along, girls.

JENNY. Oh, Miss Brodie!

LLOYD. Miss Brodie, I want to take this opportunity to thank you for your post card.

BRODIE. As Mr. Lloyd is an artist, I thought he would appreciate a card depicting one of Giotto's frescoes. Girls! It's time to go home!

LLOYD. Miss Brodie, I've finished that painting. You

know the one I mean. Would you come over to the studio Sunday and tell me what you think of it?

BRODIE. I'm . . . I have another engagement.

LLOYD. (*Confidently demanding.*) Break it.

BRODIE. I couldn't possibly. I'm . . . going to Cramond. Mr. Lowther has invited me to Cramond.

LLOYD. Mr. Lowther, the new music teacher? That Mr. Lowther?

BRODIE. Mr. Lowther . . . has a small boat. He has invited me to go sailing. (*A faint ·pause.*) This Sunday. (*Holds out her gloved hand to* LLOYD.) Good afternoon, Mr. Lloyd. We must catch the tram. Though I doubt we. shall get seats. It is nineteen-thirty-one. And chivalry is dead. (BRODIE *turns and marches off, surrounded by the* GIRLS.)

JENNY. Mr. Lloyd's wife had another baby this summer. That makes five!

SANDY. Oh, well—the Lloyds are Catholic and are made to have lots of babies—by force!

(*LIGHTS out.*)

ACT ONE

SCENE 5

SCHOOLROOM LIGHTS up.

BRODIE. Benito Mussolini is a man of action. He has made Capri a sanctuary for birds. Thousands of birds live and sing today that might well have ended their careers on a piece of toast. (LOWTHER *enters.*) Ah, Mr. Lowther. This is Mr. Lowther, the music teacher. There is a great deal Mr. Lowther can teach you about the modulation of your tones. Mr. Lowther, I entrust you with the creme de la creme. Jenny, dear, let Mr. Lowther hear your tones. (JENNY *sings.*) And I recommend Sandy to you for her vowel sounds. Sandy's mother is English. Let us hear a vowel sound, Sandy.

SANDY. Snow— Superior— Sewing.

LOWTHER. Now, girls—

BRODIE. Teach my girls something special, Mr. Lowther. Something perhaps from "Traviata." Who can translate that for me? Monica?

MONICA. The fallen woman, Miss Brodie.

BRODIE. Some of my girls are to attend the Carl Rosa performance next month.

LOWTHER. But don't you think . . . I mean "Traviata" is so— (*Blushes.*) uh—so—

BRODIE. (*Archly.*) So romantic? (*Smiles.*) Of course it is. It is *Italian!* What nobler consecration of Verdi's genius than to fire our sluggish Northern passions? Teach my girls an aria!

LOWTHER. (*His eyes wide with admiration.*) Oh! Yes. (*Now ducks his head shyly.*) But . . . perhaps I'd better —better *start off* with a march!

BRODIE. Stand up, little girls. To the music room. And walk with your heads up, up, like Sybil Thorndike. A woman of noble mien.

(LOWTHER *bursts into song.*)

LOWTHER. Page 35.
   "March, march Ettrick and Teviotdale,
    Why the de'il dinna ye march forward in order?
    March, march Eskdale and Liddledale,
    All the blue bonnets are over the border!"

(*He sets the* CHILDREN *marching out of the room, prepared to bring up the rear.*)

BRODIE. (*When most of the* CHILDREN *are well on their way.*) Mr. Lowther— (*Eagerly, he turns back toward her. So does the ever-curious* SANDY.) March on, Sandy. I must have a word with Mr. Lowther. (SANDY *obeys, but puts an elbow into* JENNY's *side to draw her attention to this interesting development they are being forced to quit.*) Mr. Lowther . . . I only wanted to ask about the possibility of renting a little boat at Cramond—

LOWTHER. Renting a boat? At Cramond?

BRODIE. Yes . . . (*Sighs.*) I thought that this Sunday I would treat myself to one last day of sun—

LOWTHER. Oh! Oh, Miss Brodie! *I* have a boat!

BRODIE. *Do* you, Mr. Lowther?

LOWTHER. It would give me the *greatest* pleasure—I mean if you would *consider* coming with *me*—

BRODIE. But, I couldn't trouble *you*, Mr. Lowther.

LOWTHER. Oh, Miss Brodie . . . I would have asked you before . . . but I didn't want to be seeming to *push* myself—*please*, Miss Brodie! Say you'll come with me!

BRODIE. (*Smiles.*) Very well. On Sunday.

LOWTHER. (*Beaming ecstatically.*) On Sunday! (*A thought.*) *After* church, of course.

BRODIE. (*Softly, graciously.*) Of course. (*He stands gazing at her, besotted.*) You must go along now, Mr. Lowther. Your *class.*

LOWTHER. Oh! (*He starts, stumbles over his own feet, smiles sheepishly.*) Sunday. You'll not forget?

BRODIE. (*Shakes her head.*) Sunday.

ACT ONE

SCENE 6

Some time later. SANDY, JENNY *and* MARY *are in the locker room.* MARY'S *portable GRAMOPHONE is softly playing music from "Traviata." Moonily,* MARY *sits listening.* SANDY *and* JENNY *listen with one ear. They are deeply concerned with a composition.*

LITTLE GIRL. Aren't you coming?

MONICA. Go along. We're busy.

LITTLE GIRL. (*Nastily.*) Oh, the creme de la creme!

SANDY. (*As she writes.*) I tremb-ling-ly . . . await
. . . you. (*Sits up, pleased.*) There.

MONICA. Read it all. From the beginning.

SANDY. Mr. Gordon Lowther, Esquire, Cramond House,
Cramond, Edinburgh, Scotland, Europe, the World. My
Dear Delightful Gordon. Your letter has moved me
deeply. But, alas, I am dedicated to my girls as is Madame
Pavlova, so—

(MISS MACKAY *enters, frowns slightly at the sound of
the gramophone, the sight of the* GIRLS. *With great
aplomb,* SANDY *pulls her composition book against
her chest, smiles serenely at* MISS MACKAY.)

MISS MACKAY. You girls should not be indoors during
recreation period. It is a fine morning. Whose gramophone
is this?

SANDY. It's Mary's, Miss Mackay.

MISS MACKAY. (*Opera is not in the Marcia Blaine
curriculum.* MACKAY *frowns.*) Well, *this* is the period for
recreation.

GIRLS. Yes, Miss Mackay.

MISS MACKAY. *Outdoor* recreation.

GIRLS. (*As* MONICA *lifts the arm from the RECORD.*)
Yes, Miss Mackay.

MISS MACKAY. (*Calls out to passing teacher.*) Miss
Campbell.

(MACKAY *nods, exits.* SANDY *moves to look down the hall
until she is certain* MACKAY *is out of hearing. Then
she comes back and carefully chooses a spot on the
RECORD to replace the needle.*)

MARY. I d—don't think we sh—shou—

SANDY. It doesn't signify what you think, Mary Mac-
Gregor.

(SANDY *and* MONICA *listen to the music and smile as it
approaches a part they like; then they softly join
in.*)

MONICA. I think we should put in something about his black eyes flashing in the moonlight.

MARY. Mr. L—Lowther's eyes aren't b—black.

SANDY. What color are his eyes?

(*The* GIRLS *look at* MARY.)

MARY. (*Confused.*) N—not *black*.

SANDY. This calls for research. Mary, go immediately to the corridor and keep watch. Mr. Lowther has to pass before the period is over. When he does, examine his eyes.

MARY. M—me?

MONICA. Go along. He might come in early.

MARY. (*Doubtfully.*) Why can't one of you go?

SANDY. Because we are the prima ballerinas and you, Mary MacGregor, are the corps de ballet.

(*Silently,* MARY *accepts this judgment, goes.*)

MONICA. Sandy—do you think Mr. Lowther is really the creme de la creme? Maybe it's Mr. Lloyd?

SANDY. The creme de la creme is *us*. "Little girls, you are going to be the creme de la creme." You lead. These are supposed to be the happiest days of our lives.

MONICA. If these are supposed to be the happiest days of our lives, why does Miss Brodie say prime is best?

SANDY. Well, she never got married like our mothers and fathers. They don't have primes.

MONICA. They have sexual intercourse.

SANDY. I don't like to think about it.

MONICA. You don't *have* to. It happens in a flash. On the spur of the moment. It happened to Teenie that works in my father's shop when she was out walking at Puddocky with her boy. They had to get married.

SANDY. You would think the urge would have passed by the time she got her *clothes* off.

MONICA. Yes, that's what I can't understand. If people take their clothes off in front of each other, it's so *rude!* They're bound to be put off their passion.

SANDY. I wouldn't like to have sexual intercourse.

MONICA. Neither would I. I'm going to be pure. Like Bonnie Kilmeny. "Kilmeny was pure as pure could be." Miss Brodie says that means she did not go to the glen in order to mix with men.

SANDY. (*She looks at her composition.*) It really is too bad if Mr. Lowther's eyes aren't black.

MONICA. Sandy, do you think Miss Brodie ever had sexual intercourse with Hugh of Flanders Field? Before he fell?

SANDY. I don't think they did anything like that. Their love was above all that.

MONICA. (*Persistently.*) Maybe. But Miss Brodie said she and Hugh clung to each other with passionate abandon on his last leave . . . but I don't think they took their clothes off. Do you?

SANDY. (*Considers this, then shakes her head.*) No. I can't see it.

(*Now, just as predicted,* MR. LOWTHER *comes down the corridor, passing* MARY. *As soon as he has passed, she comes running excitedly back to the* GIRLS.)

MARY. He came! M—Mr. Lowther! I saw h—him!

SANDY. Well? What color are his eyes?

MARY. H—his eyes?

SANDY. Mary MacGregor, you'll never be one of Life's Elite.

(*A BELL rings: the end of the recreation period.*)

LIGHTS DIM OUT

ACT ONE

SCENE 7

BRODIE *sits alone in the empty classroom, grading papers. We see* TEDDY LLOYD. *He stands in the doorway watching* BRODIE, *until she becomes conscious of his presence, turns.*

LLOYD. (*Teasing.*) Now why do you keep avoiding me when you know I'm *madly* longing to hear *all* about those wild weekends at Cramond.

BRODIE. (*Serenely.*) My girls adore Cramond. It's lovely.

LLOYD. And what about old Lowther? Is he lovely? Is his boat lovely?

BRODIE. (*Refusing to be baited.*) Mr. Lowther's boat is small. But his house is quite large, and the grounds are extensive.

LLOYD. Extensive.

BRODIE. He inherited the place from his mother.

LLOYD. I must assume he inherited his dashing, cavalier ways . . . (*Grins.*) *also* from his *mother.* Look here, I'm going out your way this afternoon. Shall we take the tram together?

BRODIE. Grazie tanto . . . I'm being given a ride by Mr. Lowther. He has a new Morris four-seater.

LLOYD. Has he indeed?

BRODIE. Yes. (*Nervously begins to take up papers, belongings, prepares to leave.*) I haven't had a chance to ask about *your* summer. Did you get away at all?

LLOYD. No, I spent the summer painting.

BRODIE. (*Sharply.*) *Family* portraits? And what have you decided to call your new daughter?

LLOYD. Diedre wants to call her Anastasia, but I'm holding out for Jean.

BRODIE. (*Quite taken aback.*) *Jean?*

LLOYD. (*Blandly.*) After an aunt of mine rumoured to make shrewd investments. (*Cruelly.*) Not unlike yourself.

BRODIE. What do you mean by that?

LLOYD. A bachelor with estates and boats and motor cars is obviously a better investment than a man with a wife and five children.

BRODIE. (*Suddenly flaring with anger.*) *Five children!* Have you never heard of Marie Stopes! Architect for Constructive Birth Control and Racial Progress!

LLOYD. (*Laughs.*) Ah, yes. An estimable woman. But

you see, my church enjoins me to go forth and be fruit-ful.

(He reaches out to touch her face. She pulls quickly back out of his reach.)

BRODIE. I am quite aware of your unfortunate affiliation with the Church of Rome! I doubt, however, whether that body gives the same interpretation to "go forth" that *you* do!

LLOYD. My church understands human imperfection and forgives it. Why can't you?

BRODIE. I am not interested in human imperfections! I am interested in Beauty! In Art! In Truth!

LLOYD. In art and beauty, maybe. In truth, no. The truth, Jean, is that you bounced into bed with the artist, but you were terrified to wake up with the man. That is the truth. I've finished your portrait, Jean. *(She doesn't answer.)* Don't you want to see it? Come back to the studio. (BRODIE *silently shakes her head.*) Why not?

BRODIE. *(The simplest statement she is ever to make. The simplest and the truest.)* You have a family. I am a teacher.

LLOYD. I had a family last July. You were a teacher last July. *(Again she shakes her head.)* If I had a pound for every time I've heard you say, "I am a teacher!" "I am a teacher! First, last, always!" *(Laughs grudgingly.)* What a firm reminder your post card was. A message from romantic Italy . . . *(Takes post card out of his pocket, reads.)* "The incomparable Giotto frescoes. How triumphantly his figures vibrate with life, casting off the formalities of decadent Byzantium! Yours truly, J. Brodie." *(Looks at her, repockets the card.)* Naturally, I was delighted to hear that old Giotto was still cocking a snoot at decadent Byzantium . . . *(Shrugs.)* That time at the studio . . . I was pleased to feel that it was *I* who enjoyed the tutorial position. *(He takes her wrist, holds it firmly. She does not move in his grasp. She is very still, seeming hardly to breathe; her eyes are fixed not on him, but on her own captive wrist.*) Come back, Jean. Come back to the studio. (*Matter-of-factly.*) You are the only sex-bestirred object in this stony pile. I *need* you.

(*Gently, he releases his hold on her. She has not moved or looked up, nor has he moved at all away from her. It is only that he has turned her loose, leaving the choice to her. There seems to be no conscious decision. It is simply that she melts compulsively, blindly into his arms. Slowly, deliberately, as if the place they are in were deeply private, they kiss. It is, as it is subsequently described, a long, lingering kiss. But now, quietly, the door opens and we see* MARY MACGREGOR'S *silly little face. Slow to take in what she is seeing, and—once she has taken it in—too slow-witted to make a getaway,* MARY *simply stands and stares, until* BRODIE, *finally aware of an alien presence, whirls around.*)

BRODIE. (*Severely.*) *Mary MacGregor.* (*Slowly, dangerously,* BRODIE *advances upon the hapless* GIRL.) Mary MacGregor . . . do you know what happened to *Peeping Tom?* (*She quotes with horrifying dramatic emphasis.*) "His eyes were shrivell'd into darkness in his head . . . and *dropt before him!"*

(*With a bleat of terror,* MARY *flees.*)

LLOYD. Hard lines on old Tom. (BRODIE *stands, worried and undecided, beside the open door.* LLOYD *moves to her and maneuvers the door closed.*) Don't worry, Jean. You've got your girls well trained. You're safe enough from that quarter. It's *me* you've got to worry about. Come back to the studio . . . (*Gently.*) Come to pose again—only to pose.

BRODIE. (*As if awaking, she starts and moves jerkily away from him.*) I will not come to the studio again.

(*Trying to pull off her usual manner, smiles brightly.*) You should paint one of my girls. Paint my Jenny. She's the pretty one.

LLOYD. Hang your girls. It's you I want to paint.

BRODIE. No.

LLOYD. Then to hell with you. (*He goes.*)

BRODIE. (*Calls gently after him.*) You really should paint Jenny, Teddy. You'll like Jenny . . . she's very pretty. . . .

LIGHTS DIM OUT

ACT ONE

SCENE 8

The locker room. Late afternoon. SANDY, JENNY *and* MONICA *are Onstage.* MARY *enters, head down, goes straight to her locker.*

SANDY. Is something wrong? (SANDY *goes to* MARY, *peers curiously at her.*) What's happened to you, Mary? Your face is all funny.

MARY. N—no, it's n—*not!*

SANDY. Yes, it is.

(MARY *tries to get past her. Curious, smelling blood, the* GIRLS *block* MARY'S *way. Suddenly, with no warning,* LLOYD *is upon them.*)

LLOYD. Ah! Miss Brodie's brood, I believe. (MARY *freezes. The* OTHER GIRLS *stare shyly at him. He stares at* MARY.) We met at the Gallery.

GIRLS. (ALL *but* MARY.) Yes, Mr. Lloyd.

(JENNY *steps boldly forward.*)

JENNY. Would you like a rosebud? (*Proffers a bag of sweets.*)

LLOYD. A what?

SANDY. It's the favourite sweet of little Princess Margaret Rose.

(LLOYD *accepts a rosebud, sucks it thoughtfully, eyeing* MARY *for a moment before turning his attention to* SANDY. *He grins, shakes his head in wonder.*)

LLOYD. Unmistakably Brodie. (*To* JENNY, *as he takes her arm and turns her about to get all angles of the face.*) And you, I suppose, are the pretty one. (*Dismissing them.*) Good afternoon, girls.

(*He gives the hangdog* MARY *one last look, grins, then moves on. The* GIRLS *watch him off. There is a weighty pause.*)

GIRLS. Good afternoon, Mr. Lloyd.

SANDY. (*Her curiosity now totally aroused.*) Mary, you are definitely upset about something.

MARY. (*Inventing desperately.*) It's m—my *brother!* I'm ups—set about m—my brother.

SANDY. You're *never* upset about your brother. But you are upset about something.

MONICA. (*Threateningly.*) Tell or I'll pinch you. *Tell.*

MARY. No! I won't tell. I love Miss Brodie and I won't tell!

SANDY. What about Miss Brodie?

MONICA. Tell or we'll shut you in the cubby again!

MARY. You wouldn't d—d—dare!

MONICA. (*Very sinister.*) Tell.

MARY. (*Bravely.*) It's n—n—none of y—your b—business— (*With the dispatch of public executioners,* MONICA *and* JENNY *grab* MARY *and push her into a small, low cupboard.*) *Please!* Please! Let m—m—me out!

(SANDY *gives a quick diabolical grin to the* OTHER GIRLS,

then gets down on her knees to speak to MARY. *Her voice a pious travesty of concern for poor* MARY.)

SANDY. Now Mary, dear . . . if something has happened to Miss Brodie, you should tell us. I'll *help* you, Mary. What have you done now?

MARY'S VOICE. She was s—s—s—so angry!

SANDY. (*Reasonably.*) Well, Mary, you know how you *are*. What have you done now?

MARY'S VOICE. N—nothing! I just w—w—went in!

JENNY. In *where?*

MARY'S VOICE. Th—the classroom.

MONICA. So?

MARY'S VOICE. So th—there th—they *were!*

SANDY. (*Patiently.*) There *who* were?

JENNY. Oh! (*Getting the picture, eyes wide, excited.*) Mr. *Lowther?* Miss Brodie and Mr. Lowther?

MARY. No! M—M—Mister L—Lloyd! Th—they were kissing!

MONICA. Mr. *Lloyd?*

SANDY. Mr. *Lloyd?*

(*She stares first at* JENNY, *then at* MONICA. *The* GIRLS *release* MARY. *Relieved to escape, grateful to her tormentors,* MARY *tells all.*)

MARY. I saw th—them! K—kissing! T—t—t—*together!* He had his arm around her.

JENNY. (*Thrilled.*) Mr. Lloyd! Mr. Lloyd's in love with Miss Brodie!

MARY. And sh—sh—she's in l—l—love with M—M—Mister Lloyd!

MONICA. What about Mr. Lowther then?

SANDY. (*Thoughtfully.*) Mr. Lloyd is an artist . . . and Miss Brodie is artistic, too. (*Judiciously.*) Perhaps Miss Brodie really loves Mr. Lloyd but he's married to another so she's working it off on Mr. Lowther. (*The* GIRLS *begin getting out their coats and hats.*) Listen, Mary. Was it a long, lingering kiss?

MARY. (*Miserably.*) I sh—sh—shouldn't h—have t—told you.

SANDY. (*Nods.*) It wasn't very elite of you. But since you did, was it a long, lingering kiss?

MARY. (*Shamefully.*) Yes.

MONICA. (*Rising, taking the center of the Stage.*) Was it like this?

(MONICA, *acting out the scene, pantomimes opening a door, then her eyes pop in a startled way as she gasps and stares. Next, she is* BRODIE *caught in* LLOYD'S *embrace, bent to his will.* MONICA'S *back to the audience as she hugs herself, her hands, on her own back, begin to travel downward, fingers wriggling with little girl prurience, downward, downward, until well-placed upon her own lower hip, one hand suddenly slaps, as if at itself. This sends the* GIRLS *into gales of laughter.* MONICA *is so overcome with success that she attempts to improve on the act by trying to run one foot up and over the calf of the other leg. This maneuver sends her crashing to the floor, but not before* MARY, *carried away, cries out:*)

MARY. That's it! That's it!

(*Before anyone knows exactly how it happened, the party has been joined by* MISS MACKAY, *who gazes coolly down at the prostrate* MONICA.)

MACKAY. It's nearly five o'clock. Time you girls were away. What were you doing, Monica?

MONICA. Just playing, Miss Mackay.

SANDY. (*Quickly.*) Playing opera.

MACKAY. Opera?

SANDY. Yes, Miss Mackay. We've been studying "Traviata."

MACKAY. Monica, show me what you were doing. (MONICA *is understandably hesitant. The* OTHER GIRLS *are stiff with horror.*) Go on. Show me.

(*Impelled by* MACKAY's *authority,* MONICA *slowly begins to embrace herself. Once the act is begun, however, she defiantly gives herself up to it, and sees it through, although nervously speeding up when she gets to the leg part. Once she is on the floor, she lies still, staring helplessly up at* MACKAY. *It is* SANDY *who comes to the rescue.*)

SANDY. She was doing Violetta expiring for love of Alfredo.

MONICA. (*Quick to back* SANDY *up.*) It's very sad.

MACKAY. (*As* MONICA *gets up.*) Rubbish! Violetta did not "expire" for love of Alfredo. Violetta was a thoroughly silly woman with diseased lungs. If she'd been properly brought up, she'd have been out on the hockey field breathing deeply. Which is precisely what you little girls should be doing. Not playacting at Italian melo-drama.

SANDY. Violetta and Alfredo were originally French.

MACKAY. How well informed you are.

MONICA. Miss Brodie took us to see "Traviata" when the Carl Rosa Company came to Edinburgh.

MACKAY. She took you to the opera?

SANDY. She takes us to concerts too, and to art galleries.

MONICA. And the theatre too. We *love* the theatre.

MACKAY. Indeed? How very good of Miss Brodie. I have been interested to see that all you Brodie girls have chosen to take the Classical Course when you move to the Senior School. You, Mary. You know your marks do not reach the required standard. Why do you want so much to go on the classical side?

MARY. M—Miss Brodie pref—prefers it.

MACKAY. It has nothing to do with Miss Brodie. I am curious as to why Miss Brodie ever singled you out, Mary. You are a fine girl, of course . . . but not—*pre-cocious.* (*A beat.*) Now I know that your guardian, Mr. Ealing, makes you a very generous allowance and it occurs to me . . . perhaps it is *you,* Mary, who occasionally treats Miss *Brodie* to the theatre? It is pleasant to have the means to treat our friends, isn't it?

MARY. (*Blushing miserably.*) B—but—Mr. Lowther p—p—paid for us to s—see "T—T—Traviata."

MACKAY. Mr. Lowther paid for you. Well, it is most kind of Mr. Lowther. I hope you are appreciative.

MARY. Oh, y—yes!

MACKAY. And you, Monica, as regards the Classical Course, you will have to earn your way in life. And your interest in the drama won't prepare you for that. A secretarial course is what you should aim for, my dear.

(MONICA *turns away, deeply offended.*)

JENNY. Miss Brodie says the foundation of real education is the Humanities. They train us to think beyond the narrow life. They train us for heroic action.

MACKAY. Heroic action? The Humanities, the Arts, Music. (*A brief pause.*) Miss Brodie is *very musical.*

SANDY. (*Boldly.*) I think Miss Brodie is more interested in art, Miss Mackay.

MACKAY. What makes you think Miss Brodie prefers art to music, Sandy?

SANDY. She told us so. Music is an interest to her but painting is a passion. (MACKAY *stares fixedly at her.* SANDY *defends herself.*) Miss Brodie *said.*

MACKAY. A passion?

SANDY. Compared to music.

MACKAY. (*Turns her inquiry on* MARY.) Now Mary, I'm sure you are too young to have passions, what are *your* cultural interests?

MARY. (*Nervously.*) S—stories?

MACKAY. Does Miss Brodie tell you stories?

MARY. Oh yes! L—love—love— (*A ferocious poke in the back by* MONICA, *and threatening looks from* SANDY *and* JENNY, *bring* MARY *to her senses. She manages to whisper hoarsely:*) Lovely s—stories!

MACKAY. Umm. Stories like "Traviata"?

SANDY. (*Quickly.*) Stories of history.

JENNY. (*Only an echo behind.*) *History.*

MONICA. Miss Brodie makes history seem like—like the *cinema.*

SANDY. (*Again quickly, attempting to rectify what may have been a mistake on* MONICA's *part.*) Not the cinema. More like *Shakespeare.*

JENNY. (*Nodding.*) Shakespeare.

MONICA. Shakespeare.

MARY. Shakespeare.

MACKAY. (*Gives them a long look; their closing of ranks is not lost on her. She sighs.*) My, my! What would we do without Miss Brodie. I could wish your arithmetic papers were better. You will have to work hard at ordinary humble subjects for your leaving certificate. Culture cannot compensate for lack of hard knowledge.

GIRLS. No, Miss Mackay.

MACKAY. I am happy to see you are devoted to Miss Brodie. But your loyalty is also due to the school.

GIRLS. Yes, Miss Mackay.

MACKAY. (*She starts off, talking as she moves toward the exit.*) I am always impressed by Miss Brodie's girls. (*A long pause.*) In one way or another.

(*There is a heavy silence after* MACKAY's *exit. All the* GIRLS *turn toward* SANDY, *whose face is a study.*)

JENNY. What are you thinking about?

SANDY. About Miss Brodie. And Mr. Lloyd.

JENNY. And Mr. Lowther? Don't forget Mr. Lowther. She goes to Cramond every Sunday.

MONICA. So do we.

SANDY. But she never comes home when we do.

MONICA. First he puts out the light. Then their toes touch . . . Then Miss Brodie—

(GIRLS *giggle.*)

SANDY. (*Her eyes narrow as she tries to visualize the*

scene.) Mr. Lowther's legs are so much longer than Miss Brodie's. He would have to wind his around hers . . .

JENNY. (*Whispering.*) Miss Brodie says, "Darling!" '
She says—

SANDY. "Mr. Lowther, you are the creme de la creme!"

(*The* GIRLS *laugh wildly.*)

JENNY. *Still* . . . (*Looks wisely at* SANDY.) They might have a baby.

SANDY. We'll have to watch Miss Brodie's stomach.

(*Having issued this ukase,* SANDY *turns and smartly marches out, followed by* JENNY, *then* MONICA, *then* MARY *on whom the lights go out, only to segue quickly up on* MISS BRODIE, *crossing to* MISS MACKAY'S *office.*)

LIGHTS OUT ON LOCKER ROOM

ACT ONE

SCENE 9

The office of MISS MACKAY. *There is a desk and chair for the* HEADMISTRESS *and another chair facing her across the desk. There is the same picture of Stanley Baldwin and a bowl of chrysanthemums.* MISS MACKAY *is alone in the room when the lights come up. She is somewhat distracted, as much as she is ever likely to be, tapping a pencil against the desktop. There is a KNOCK at the door.* MISS MACKAY *straightens up and adjusts her face.* BRODIE *enters with a poised smile.*

BRODIE. (*Glancing at her watch.*) I hope I'm not late. (*A pause.*) Or early.

MACKAY. No! It's 4:15 precisely. You are most punctilious. Thank you for finding the time. Please sit down. My, my! You do wear such *stimulating* colors.

BRODIE. My credo is stimulate, enliven, uplift.

MACKAY. No doubt. But the Marcia Blaine School is essentially conservative and any conservative school must turn out pupils who can read and write and add up. (*Smiles.*) I have observed, Miss Brodie, some of your girls counting on their fingers.

BRODIE. (*Also smiling.*) Miss Mackay, have you summoned me to your eyrie to suggest that I am unqualified to impart the mysteries of multiplication?

MACKAY. Certainly not. (*She continues to smile, refusing to seem intolerant.*) I merely want to point out that we are not what, I believe, is called a progressive school. We do not encourage the—uh—progressive attitudes. Now I have noticed, Miss Brodie, a—a spirit of precocity among your girls. Your special girls.

BRODIE. (*Quickly blocking* MACKAY's *move.*) Why, *thank you.* I am in my prime and my girls are benefiting from it. I am proud to think that my girls are perhaps more—aware.

MACKAY. (*Pouncing.*) Precisely.

BRODIE. (*Before* MACKAY *can pursue this line of thought.*) To me education is a leading out. The word education comes from the root ex meaning out and duco, I lead. To me, education is simply a leading out of what is already there.

MACKAY. (*Dryly.*) I had hoped there might also be a certain amount of putting *in.*

BRODIE. (*Bravely, foolishly, plunging on.*) That would not be education but intrusion. From the root prefix "in" meaning "in" and the stem "trudo," "I thrust." Ergo to thrust a lot of information into a pupil's head.

MACKAY. (*Sighs deeply.*) To discuss education with such a dedicated teacher is always instructive. But it was not for that I asked you to come here. Miss Brodie.

(*Directly.*) I am told that you make weekly expeditions to Cramond.

BRODIE. Yes. Isn't it a lovely spot?

MACKAY. It is indeed. I believe Mr. Lowther inherited the estate from his mother. He has lived there all his life. Overprotected, perhaps. He is not a worldly man. Not a reckless man. I doubt if he would even recognize recklessness in others. And recklessness is an indulgence which we at Marcia Blaine must eschew. Not only within our walls, but in the personal life—the conduct, as it were—of our teaching staff.

(*A moment of silence. Then gently,* BRODIE *speaks.*)

BRODIE. I do not believe I have ever fully appreciated the taxing load of trivia with which a headmistress must concern herself.

MACKAY. With which we must both concern ourselves. Appearances must be considered. Your—visits to Crammond Sunday after Sunday might invite ungenerous gossip in that small community.

BRODIE. I must confess I am astonished, astonished that anyone, anyone at all, might misconstrue my visits to Cramond. I am always chaperoned by my girls. Miss Mackay, I do not believe that you would ever give serious attention to the ignorant gossip of ignorant people. It is on your good judgment both as an administrator and as a *woman* that I must rely, that I *do* rely.

MACKAY. (*Dryly.*) I appreciate your confidence in me, Miss Brodie, but I am responsible to my school's Board of Governors.

BRODIE. I flatter myself that I am not unknown to the board—having been a member of the staff of Marcia Blaine some six years prior to *your* engagement. I feel quite safe in saying that no *member of the board* has *ever* shown anything but approval and appreciation of my teaching methods. (*Laughs lightly.*) Miss Mackay. I *use* Cramond. As I use anything than can possibly be of benefit to my girls. I use the woods of Cramond for lessons in botany . . . the rocks of the shore to investigate the mysteries of geology . . . It was from Cramond that Agricola's fleet set sail for the first circumnavigation of Britain. It should be patently clear to the Board of Governors that my expeditions there are expeditions for enrichment—enrichment both for my girls and for Marcia Blaine. (*Gives a brilliant smile.*)

(*A long pause.* MACKAY *sees that there is no present way around this mountain of security. She sighs.*)

MACKAY. Well, thank you, Miss Brodie. I'm sure we've come to understand each other a good deal better.

BRODIE. (*She stands, triumphant.*) I am always at your command, Miss Mackay.

MACKAY. (*Dryly.*) Thank you. Good day, Miss Brodie.

BRODIE. (*Stops to gaze at flowers.*) Chrysanthemums. Such *serviceable* flowers. (*A brilliant smile, exits.*)

MACKAY. (*She broods after* BRODIE, *finally stirs to pick up one of several books on her desk. She opens the book and begins to search for some reference. She finds it, smiles grimly, reads aloud.*) "Educere, to lead. *Educari,* to feed." *Ergo*, Miss Brodie, to educate does not mean to lead out—it means to *feed*—to feed *in*. (*Snaps book shut.*) It would seem that your Latin is as "progressive" as your mathematics. Now just what *is* your subject, Miss *Brodie?* (*There is a set and determined look on her face.*)

LIGHTS DOWN SLOWLY

ACT ONE

SCENE 10

The lawn in front of the school.

SANDY. "I shall place the baby in the care of a worthy shepherd . . ." (*Erases, rewrites.*) "I shall place the *infant* in the care of a worthy shepherd and his wife."

MONICA. Peachy!

SANDY. (*Smugly.*) It's shaping up.

MONICA. It's so much better since *Mr. Lloyd.*

SANDY. Well, it's a real triangle, you see.

McCREADY. (*A gardener, enters pushing wheelbarrow.*) Miss Mackay's orders. Nae sitting on the grass after hours.

MONICA. We have an engagement with Miss Brodie. Right here on *this grass.* (MR. McCREADY *snorts angrily, putters suspiciously about for a moment, then moves on, leaving the wheelbarrow near the* GIRLS. MONICA *eyes him cautiously for a moment, then returns to the composition, reading over* SANDY'S *shoulder.*) *I've* got an idea— (*Tries to take the paper from* SANDY.)

SANDY. No—let me finish—

MONICA. It's my turn! (*Writes furiously.*)

SANDY. Oh, I say! (*Reads, claps her hands.*) *Marvelous!* Oh, that's *it!* That's *it!*

(*We now hear* BRODIE'S *voice followed shortly by* BRODIE *herself, and the* OTHER TWO GIRLS. *During the time it takes them to get on Stage,* SANDY *snatches up the letter and hurriedly disposes of it among the gardening props.*)

BRODIE. Fresh air, forsooth! If we breathe in any more chalk dust, we shall all be found strewn upon the floor like fatalities in a Fife pit disaster!

(BRODIE *has come equipped with a parasol, while* MARY

and MONICA *are lugging two picnic baskets, a camp stool and a blanket.*)

GIRLS. Hello, Miss Brodie.

(*Joining* SANDY *and* JENNY, *they* ALL *busy themselves, spreading the blanket, setting up the camp stool for* BRODIE, *examining the contents of the baskets.*)

BRODIE. Refreshment al fresco! Enough to go around but the lion's share for Mr. Lowther. I am going to fatten Mr. Lowther up. A full half-stone before the holidays. It is my pledge. Now, girls . . . (SANDY, JENNY *and* MARY *examine the contents of the picnic baskets. After a moment.*) Little girls . . . did I neglect to tell you that once on leave from the war, Hugh took me out sailing in a fishing boat . . . We spent our happiest time among the rocks and pebbles of a small seaport . . . Sometimes Hugh would sing—he had a rich tenor voice . . . (*The sound of the MUSIC swells for one short passage, we hear* LOWTHER'S *voice, alone, then it fades. The MUSIC dies, trembling.* BRODIE'S *voice lowers, intimately.*) At other times he would set up his easel and paint. (*There is a silence now upon them as Hugh the painter is invoked.*) Hugh was—he was very talented at both arts. Though I think—I think the painter was the real Hugh . . . (*A sly and knowing look is exchanged between* SANDY *and* JENNY. *Oblivious,* BRODIE *sighs, pulls her attention back to the* GIRLS, *gazes proudly at them.*) But you girls are my life now. I am the potter and you are my pride. Give me a girl at an impressionable age and she is mine for life— (*We see* LOWTHER *come hurrying out to join them.*) You girls are shaping up. Already I can discern— uh!

(LOWTHER *hurries to present himself to* BRODIE *like a small boy, all spruced and polished for an audience with a tolerant and loving grown-up.*)

LOWTHER. I knew you must be waiting—

BRODIE. Here comes our Mr. Lowther.

GIRLS. Hello, Mr. Lowther.

BRODIE. Our minstrel sweet . . . "Oh synge unto me roundelaie, Oh droppe the brynie tear wythe mee, da da de da, da da de da and like a running river be . . . poor doomed young Chatterton . . ." (*Gives* LOWTHER *a radiant smile.*) Now, Mr. Lowther, you must cooperate in the fattening project—half a stone. It will enrich your voice . . . Caruso has the appetite of a giant! (*Hums LA DONNA MOBILE as she distributes tea.*) What shall I make for Sunday's tea? Shall I make a lobster salad? Or some of the pate de fois gras sandwiches you girls like?

LOWTHER. (*The small boy.*) I should like a Chester cake—

BRODIE. (*Sternly.*) There is no nourishment in sugar.

LOWTHER. (*Pleased to be refused his cake.*) What good care you take of me.

BRODIE. Of course.

(*She gives* LOWTHER *food; he leans toward her, lowers his voice in a futile attempt to exclude the* GIRLS.)

LOWTHER. I was—noticed. At "Traviata." I was noticed. And reported to Mr. Gaunt.

BRODIE. Mr. Gaunt? You mean the minister at Cramond? Whatever for?

LOWTHER. One of the elders of the church— (*He offers this to her like a bouquet.*) considered La Traviata—that is the *story* of La Traviata—he said that the choirmaster of his church had no business attending that sort of thing. With an unmarried lady. And children. (BRODIE *leans back the better to stare at him with disbelief. Proudly.*) Oh, I defended myself! Fiercely!

BRODIE. Girls! There has been an attempt to persecute Mr. Lowther on our account! He has been reproached for escorting us to "Traviata"! (*The* GIRLS *stare, impressed. Sternly.*) One must never succumb to provincial ignorance. Mr. Lowther did not, nor . . . (*A riveting look at the* GIRLS.) shall anyone under *my* tutelage! Eat up, Mr. Lowther! (SANDY, *reaching for an extra biscuit, glances up. She hesitates, her eyes apparently caught by some movement at an upper window.*) What is it, Sandy?

SANDY. I think Miss Mackay has been watching us from her window.

BRODIE. (*A swift upward glance.*) Indeed! I wonder how many more picnics we shall be allowed before Miss Mackay thinks to patrol the grounds? Mr. Lowther! (BRODIE *now defiantly takes a sandwich from the basket and with infinite tenderness feeds* LOWTHER *from her own hand, then she leans towards him and possessively smooths his shirt collar, smiling all the time as provocatively as a siren. Now she turns to include the* GIRLS, *who have watched all this with fascination.* BRODIE'S *eyes sweep around the circle, claiming every soul for her own. And then, in tight control of her little world, she looks again toward* MACKAY'S *window, gives a gracious little wave of fingers and a taunting smile.*) I told you of our latest interview. She made our appointment for four-fifteen. Not four or four-thirty, but four-fifteen! She thought to intimidate me by the use of quarter hours!

MONICA. (*Breathless.*) Do you really think Miss Mackay wants to drive you out of Marcia Blaine?

BRODIE. Ha! It does not *signify* what Miss Mackay wants. Here I am, and here I stay! I would not leave you girls for the Lord L—

SANDY. (*Slyly eyeing* LOWTHER *who was not included in* BRODIE'S *passionate avowal.*) Lord Lyon King-of-Arms?

BRODIE. Not even he! Eat up, Mr. Lowther. Co-operation is the keynote. (*She is suddenly very gay.*) Jenny, do us a fling for comic relief. (*Gracefully,* JENNY *begins a spirited fling.* SANDY *gets up, joins* JENNY *in the dance,* SANDY'S *efforts are not up to* JENNY'S, *but she labors mightily to please* MISS BRODIE. *At last the* TWO CHILDREN *breathlessly come back to the blanket,* SANDY *to fling herself at* BRODIE'S *feet,* JENNY *to take her ease at the edge of the blanket—slightly removed from the* OTHERS.) Brava! Brava! (*She flings the lilac spray to* JENNY, *ignoring the less successful but more strenuous efforts of* SANDY.) Archibrava! (*Her smile circles the* GROUP, *it is* hers.) These are *my* girls, Mr. Lowther. Forsooth, they are the *Brodie* girls! Monica is histrionic. She will perform in plays—or perhaps write them. One day we shall *pay* to see Monica. (BRODIE'S *eye lights on lumpen* MARY, *stolidly consuming a banana.* BRODIE *sighs with frustration.*) Mary MacGregor is alone in the world. Her needs are great. (*Her hand falls possessively on* MARY'S *shoulder.* MARY *gives up the banana to gaze adoringly at* BRODIE. *Smiles reassuringly at the* CHILD.) That is what *I* am for—to help Mary MacGregor find her way. I shall devote my energies to Mary. She will stop stuttering . . . She will—*brisk up* . . . Mary MacGregor will distinguish herself. For *me*. I have no doubt. (*Shyly* MARY *beams; her hand goes out, satisfied to touch Miss* BRODIE'S *skirt.* BRODIE *smiles at her, then her glance turns to* JENNY. *Her smile intensifies; the sight of* JENNY *invariably brings a smile to* BRODIE'S *face; it is a smile, somehow, of self-pleasure.*) Then there is Jenny. Sometimes I feel that . . . there is a *spiritual* bond between Jenny and me. I don't expect Jenny feels this yet . . . but someday she will. (JENNY *smiles, accepting all,* expecting *all, as her beauty has taught her to. She is not smug, just sensible of her beauty and its value.*) Jenny will be beautiful and have animal magnetism. Already she has caught the eye of an artist. Mr. Lloyd remarked her—unusual quality! What was it he said, Sandy?

SANDY. (*With a touch of sullenness.*) All he said was, "And you, I suppose, are the pretty one."

BRODIE. Jenny has a profile of deceptive purity. And Sandy—Sandy—

SANDY. Sandy is famous for her vowel sounds.

BRODIE. (*Stares at* SANDY *a moment, then smiles.*) And

you are very *dependable,* Sandy. *Very* dependable. (*Gives* SANDY *a careless pat.*) Now. Monica—recite for us, please.

MONICA. What shall I recite, Miss Brodie?

BRODIE. Something—something of magic.

MONICA. (*Not at all coy, but very pleased to entertain.*)

"There she weaves by night and day
A magic web with colors gay.
She has heard a whisper say
A curse is on her if she stay
    To look down on Camelot.

"She knows not what the curse may be—"

(*At the repetition of the word "curse," JENNY collapses in smothered giggles. As cross as she is, SANDY is forced to snicker. Even MONICA, at the cost of her performance, cannot resist the implication. A hand goes over her grinning mouth.*)

BRODIE. (*Severely.*) Mr. Lowther, the Philistines are upon us. (*Slowly rising, commanding silence, attention, even reverence, BRODIE, herself, takes up the recitation.*)

"She knows not what the curse may be,
And so she weaveth steadily,
And little other care hath she
    The Lady of Shalott."

It lifts one up. (*Simply, unselfconsciously, BRODIE pauses, her hand thrust upward from her breast.*) Where there is no vision, the people perish. (*Excited, SANDY moves now as close to BRODIE as she can get. The emotion that BRODIE herself feels is most clearly mirrored in SANDY's upturned attentive face.*)

"But in her web she still delights
To weave the mirror's magic sights,
For often through the silent nights
A funeral, with plumes and lights,
    And music went to Camelot;

"Or when the moon was overhead,
Came two young lovers lately wed;
'I am half sick of shadows,' said
The Lady of Shalott."

(There is a brief, breathless silence, then, slightly off to one side, away from the OTHERS, JENNY *stretches senselessly onto her back, the lilac spray across her breast.)*

JENNY. *(Repeating softly, rhythmically, hypnotically, feeling only a* physical *response to the poetry.)* ". . . The *Lady of* Sha*lott!"*

*(*BRODIE *turns in the direction of* JENNY, *heedlessly disengages herself of* SANDY, *moves a step or two toward* JENNY *to gaze down on the* CHILD. BRODIE *smiles secretly. Her voice is almost a whisper in the pale gloom of late day.)*

BRODIE. *Yes.* Jenny will be painted many times. (SANDY *watches* BRODIE *with jealous longing. Brodie watches* JENNY. JENNY *watches the sky.)* I think perhaps . . . that Jenny . . . I think that Jenny will be famous for—sex . . .

*(*LOWTHER *smiles permissively up at the daring* MISS BRODIE. *The* GIRLS, *however, turn to stare at* JENNY, *one of their own number, about whom their infallible* MISS BRODIE *has just made such an astonishing prediction.* MONICA *and* MARY *are simply amazed.* SANDY *eyes first* JENNY *and then* BRODIE. *Her eyes narrow. Whatever her reaction, there is surely nothing simple about it. The LIGHTS pinpoint* SANDY, MISS BRODIE *and* JENNY.)*

THE LIGHTS FADE SLOWLY, SLOWLY

ACT TWO

Scene 1

LIGHTS up on CONVENT GARDEN.

MR. PERRY. Tell me, Sister, was your Miss Brodie a Catholic?

HELENA. No, Miss Brodie disapproved of the Church of Rome. She said it was for people who did not want to think for themselves.

MR. PERRY. But you, most demonstratively, think for yourself. And you are a Catholic convert.

HELENA. Yes.

MR. PERRY. But you said that Miss Brodie was a great influence on your life.

HELENA. Miss Brodie was a romantic. Her rejection of truth was so extreme that it created in me a reverse hunger.

MR. PERRY. At what age?

HELENA. Oh, at a very early age.

MR. PERRY. And did you trust yourself—at such an early age—to define "truth"?

HELENA. Let us just say that I rejected Miss Brodie's "truth."

MR. PERRY. And, has the rejection that you made as a child remained valid for you all these years?

HELENA. Why shouldn't it?

MR. PERRY. Because a child's view is so—fractional— so illusional.

HELENA. Even as a child, Mr. Perry, I had very little patience with the illusional—a child has eyes; a child has ears—and the ability to reason.

MR. PERRY. Ah! What a—dangerous young person you must have been.

HELENA. I? It was not *I* who was dangerous!

LIGHTS DIM OUT

ACT TWO

SCENE 2

The time is three years later. The BRODIE GIRLS *are now fourteen.*

When the LIGHTS come up, we first see BRODIE *and* LOWTHER. *It is a raw, rainy Edinburgh day.* LOWTHER *carries several large bundles of groceries.* BRODIE *carries an umbrella.* LOWTHER *looks perfectly miserable.*

BRODIE. I shall cook the salmon tonight . . . I want to be free to spend as much time tomorrow as possible with the girls. I simply cannot get used to not having them in my class this year— (*Catches sight of* LOWTHER'S *face.*) Oh, Gordon, what *is* the matter with you? Why are you sulking *now?*

LOWTHER. That was no proper way to speak to the greengrocer, Jean!

BRODIE. Do your bourgeois attitudes forbid a political discussion with one's greengrocer?

LOWTHER. I don't see anything political about—what you were talking about.

BRODIE. (*Serenely.*) Birth control, as I told Mr. Geddes, is very much a political issue for the working classes. (LOWTHER *cringes. Suddenly* BRODIE *stops, stares ahead.*) Isn't that Sandy? (*Calls out.*) Sandy! Sandy!

SANDY. Hello, Miss Brodie. Hello, Mr. Lowther.

BRODIE. What a surprise. I thought you and Jenny were attending some sort of social gathering? Where is Jenny?

SANDY. (*Uneasily.*) I'm—going to meet Jenny. Now.

BRODIE. I see. (*There is some secret here.* BRODIE *feels it, is puzzled.*) Well. Mr. Lowther and I have been shopping for tomorrow . . . I shall make a Charlotte Russe especially for you girls. How I look forward to seeing all of you together. I do miss you.

SANDY. We miss you too, Miss Brodie.

BRODIE. We have much to discuss.

LOWTHER. Please, Miss Brodie.

BRODIE. I want to tell you about the new plot afoot to force me to resign. Certain teachers have taken to bidding me good morning in the corridors with predestination in their smiles! It has been suggested that I apply for a post at one of the progressive, that is to say, crank schools. I shall *not* apply for a post at a crank school. I shall not resign! If they want to get rid of me, they will have to—

SANDY. Assassinate you.

BRODIE. (*Looks at* SANDY; *laughs, pleased.*) *Precisely!*

SANDY. (*She grins back delightedly.*) Miss Brodie . . .

BRODIE. Yes.

SANDY. It was supposed to be a secret. I'm going to Mr. Lloyd's studio. The others will be there too. Jenny is sitting for Mr. Lloyd. He began painting her this summer.

BRODIE. (*Riveted.*) Jenny is sitting for Mr. Lloyd! And *I* was not to know?

SANDY. It was just to—make a surprise. I shouldn't have told you . . . but I thought you'd be so pleased—

BRODIE. (*Gives* SANDY *a long speculative look.*) Indeed. Indeed I am pleased. (*Smiles.*) Thank you, Sandy. You are developing into a girl of great insight. You know, Sandy, I should be most interested in hearing *your own* impressions about—Jenny's portrait—but we mustn't discuss it tomorrow when the others are there—as you say, it is to be a surprise . . . Monday. Monday, bring your golf clubs to school and we shall use our lunch hour to practice our swings. In the gymnasium. Just the two of us. Sandy, dear, I had forgotten how much I could depend on you.

SANDY. (*She grins happily, turns and runs off. Over her shoulder.*) Goodbye, Miss Brodie— Goodbye, Mr. Lowther—see you tomorrow! (*She is gone.*)

(*For a moment* BRODIE *stands, looking after the girl.*

LOWTHER *is totally forgotten. No part of the um- brella covers him.*)

LOWTHER. *Please*, Jean . . . I'm all wet and my arms are cramped—I've been carrying all this—

BRODIE. (*Turns, begins to stride briskly along.*) Really, Gordon. What do you expect? No gentleman would be seen dead carrying bundles in the public streets . . . (*He trots after her as:*)

LIGHTS DIM OUT

ACT TWO

SCENE 3

We are in TEDDY LLOYD'S *studio.* JENNY, *draped in a swath to chiffon over her clothes that both flows and clings, is posed in profile.* LLOYD *is painting her.* MONICA *and* MARY *are present.*

LLOYD. Personally, I've always wondered at the endur- ing attractions of Cramond. How long have all of you been trudging out there?

MONICA. Three years.

LLOYD. My God!

JENNY. There's always lovely food at Cramond.

MARY. Miss Brodie cooks.

LLOYD. What are Miss Brodie's specialiteés?

MONICA. Lasagne Verde, Risotto a la Milanese.

MARY. Harlot Russe.

MONICA. *Charlotte* Russe!

MARY. Charlotte Russe.

LLOYD. No wonder old Lowther's come to look like a fatted calf. All that rich food will give him a stoppage.

JENNY. Not if he eats his greens.

MONICA. Miss Brodie is very good to Mr. Lowther. He couldn't do without her.

MARY. Sh—she w—w—watches his health.

LLOYD. Yes? And what does Mr. Lowther do for Miss Brodie?

SANDY. (*Who has entered silently and is taking off her coat.*) He sings to her.

MONICA and JENNY. Hello, Sandy.

(LLOYD *turns to stare at what is possibly pure impudence;* SANDY *returns his look, at first, ingenuously blank, then with a smile that cannot be* proved *lacking in innocence.* LLOYD *snorts, goes back to painting.*)

LLOYD. Put that wet thing someplace else.

MONICA. (*Who has been pawing through a stack of paintings among the many piled against the wall.*) Why, it's Miss Brodie! (*Then some doubt.*) Isn't it? But the hair is dark—

LLOYD. (*Looking over.*) That's the very first study I did of Jenny—

MONICA. (*Sycophantically.*) Oh—oh, of course. Of course it's Jenny. How silly of me. It's much more like Jenny. It's terribly like her.

SANDY. All the studies of Jenny look like Miss Brodie. (*Again* LLOYD *looks at her. Defensively, she insists.*) *I* think they do.

LLOYD. And what do you think of the work in progress? Does it too resemble Miss Brodie?

SANDY. There is a resemblance now that you mention it.

LLOYD. (*He studies the painting.*) It makes Jenny look rather mature.

SANDY. We're *all* rather mature.

LLOYD. Some people at school think you're too mature.

MONICA. (*Smugly.*) Everybody's jealous because they know we have more fun . . . We go places and do things like going to Cramond—

LLOYD. And hanging about an artist's studio. Very glamorous.

SANDY. Miss Brodie is glamorous. Don't you think she is?

JENNY. In Egypt when her dragoman came to the train to see her off, he brought her a huge bouquet of flowers.

LLOYD. Did he now?

SANDY. (*Sharply.*) Don't you believe it?

LLOYD. (*Smiles.*) Of course I do. (*Looks at her.*) Don't you?

SANDY. (*Coolly.*) Miss Brodie is in her prime.

MONICA. (*Shocked at a picture she has unearthed.*) Oh!

(LLOYD *turns, sees the picture before she can put it out of sight.*)

LLOYD. (*Calmly.*) Wherever did you find him? I painted him in my student days. That is called a "life study." I had a difficult time with pectoral muscles.

SANDY. Pectoral?

LLOYD. Chest.

MONICA. (*In relief.*) *Oh!*

SANDY. (*Disgusted.*) Oh, Monica.

MONICA. What?

SANDY. Miss Brodie says that anyone of a cultured home and heritage makes no fuss about the human body.

MONICA. (*Quickly flaring up.*) Who's making any fuss?

SANDY. You are.

LLOYD. Mary . . . (MARY *snaps guiltily into focus.*) What's new on the rialto, Mary?

MARY. Th—the wh—what?

LLOYD. How's your brother? How is he progressing at Oxford?

MARY. (*Her eyes dart nervously.*) His tutor c—c—caught f—fire!

SANDY. *Caught fire?* The *tutor?* (MARY *nods.*) How? From what?

MARY. F—from my brother!

JENNY. (*Convulsed.*) Your brother set fire to the tutor!
(*She is beside herself at the notion.*)

(SANDY *and* MONICA *are* outraged. *Sound of distant*
ROAR.)

LLOYD. The one o'clock gun already! I think that's
enough for today, Jenny. If I keep on I shall ruin the
mouth. And that would be a pity. (JENNY *instantly jumps
down from the pose and hastens to examine the painting.*) What do you think?

SANDY. (*As the* GIRLS *crowd around.*) Miss Brodie says
Jenny has a profile of deceptive purity.

LLOYD. And what does she say about you?

SANDY. That my eyes are too small.

MONICA. (*Spitefully.*) And so they are.

JENNY. When shall I come back?

LLOYD. Oh, next weekend. Whenever you have time.

JENNY. Come on, Sandy. I'm *famished!*

SANDY. No, I've only just arrived. Besides, I have to
go straight home—my mother is expecting me.

MONICA. Oh, your eternal mother!

MARY. G—g—goodbye, Mr. L—Lloyd. B—bye, S—
Sandy— (*She is yanked out by* MONICA.)

(*Now the* GIRLS *are gone, leaving* SANDY *and* LLOYD
alone. SANDY *holds her ground.*)

SANDY. (*Examining another of* LLOYD'S *paintings.*) Is
this your family?

LLOYD. Myself, my wife, and all the kiddies.

(SANDY *picks up the canvas he indicates, examines it
closely. He waits for her to comment.*)

SANDY. Is your wife in her prime?

LLOYD. (*Smiles.*) Perhaps not yet.

SANDY. (*Stares her insolent, blackmailing stare.*) I
didn't think so.

LLOYD. One day I would like to paint all you Brodie girls, and see what sort of group portrait I could make of you.

SANDY. (*Glancing back at the family portrait.*) We'd look like one great big Brodie, I suppose.

LLOYD. You're a clever little cat, aren't you? (*She only stares unblinkingly at him. LLOYD does not quite know what to make of this girl, so he follows his instinct. With no warning whatever, he catches her by the arm, pulls her to him and kisses her. Quite thoroughly.*) That'll teach you to look at an artist like that. (SANDY *starts to run for the door, wiping her mouth with the back of her hand. Before she reaches the door, she realizes that she has left behind her book bag. She turns, spots it, but won't risk approaching* LLOYD *to retrieve it. He sees her dilemma, grabs up the bag, laughs, pitches it to her.*) You want your coat too? Don't worry, girl. You're just about the plainest little thing I've ever seen in my life.

(*Instead of letting* SANDY *leave,* LLOYD *goes, leaving the* GIRL *alone in the studio, still vigorously wiping away at her mouth.*)

LIGHTS DOWN

ACT TWO

SCENE 4

Monday. The gymnasium. A body of GIRLS *engaged in drill under the supervision of* MISS CAMPBELL *and her whistle. At the end of the exercise,* ALL *collapse on the floor.* MISS CAMPBELL *gives them five seconds, then blows the whistle again; the* GIRLS *stagger to their feet.*

CAMPBELL. Dismissed.

(*Groaning, calling to each other, the* GROUP *disperses, leaving* JENNY *and* MARY. JENNY, *because she wants to play a moment on the rings;* MARY, *because she feels obliged to stand and wait for* JENNY. *Enter* BRODIE *and* SANDY, *carrying golf clubs.*)

BRODIE. Jenny!

JENNY and MARY. Hullo, Miss Brodie. H—h—hello, M—Miss B—Brodie!

BRODIE. (*As* JENNY *executes a maneuver on the ropes which stretches her arms back, causing her young breasts to strain against her shirt.* BRODIE *smiles complacently at the sight of* JENNY'S *beauty.*) Jenny is like a heroine from a novel by Mr. D. H. Lawrence. She has got instinct. When you are seventeen or eighteen, Jenny, you will come to the moment of your great fulfillment.

JENNY. (*Placidly.*) Yes, honestly I think so, Miss Brodie.

BRODIE. You will know love.

JENNY. Yes, I expect so.

BRODIE. (*Smiles indulgently.*) How pleasant it was yesterday having you girls together again at Cramond. (*Sighs.*) It is seeing you all together that one misses. Ah, well. (*Reluctant to let them go.*) Now that you have graduated into a world of highly trained specialists—that is to say, teachers who've chosen to limit themselves to one subject—perhaps I can learn from you. I should like to study Greek. You girls can take turns instructing me . . . Who amongst you is the most promising in the study of Greek?

JENNY. (*Cheerfully.*) Oh, Sandy, of course. Sandy's a brain.

BRODIE. Very well, Sandy shall begin. John Stuart Mill used to rise at dawn to learn Greek at the age of five, and what John Stuart Mill could do as an infant at dawn, I can do on a Saturday afternoon in my prime.

(JENNY, *suddenly reverting to childhood, lets go of the*

rings and lands with a heavy, awkward thud on the gymnasium floor, scrambles up cheerfully, pulls MARY *along after her.*)

JENNY. Come along.

MARY. Wh—wh—why?

JENNY. (*Grins at* SANDY, *teases.*) Because we aren't *wanted.* (*Echoing* SANDY's *constant refrain to* MARY.) You *know* how Sandy *is!*

(*To a baleful look from* SANDY, JENNY *drags* MARY *off. Very faintly, from a distance, we hear the* CHOIR *practice. The sound is intermittently there throughout the following scene, though never obtrusive.*)

BRODIE. (*Still concentrating on* JENNY, *unmindful of* SANDY's *jealousy.*) Have you noticed, Sandy, how Jenny has altered? She seems older.

SANDY. (*Sullenly.*) *I'm* older, too.

BRODIE. (*Carelessly, as she grips her golf club.*) Of course you are, dear. But—*Jenny* has *developed.*

SANDY. Well, she has got the change.

BRODIE. Educated women refer to that function of nature as the menarche. (*Swings expertly.* SANDY *tries to imitate* BRODIE's *style.*) *Now.* Tell me about Mr. Lloyd. And Jenny's portrait. Is it beautiful?

SANDY. (*Shrugs; this is not, after all, what she would like to discuss.*) It's all right.

BRODIE. Your wrists, Sandy. Remember your wrists.

(*There is a moment of silence while the* TWO *continue to swing, taking out in physical exertion their irritation and disappointment in each other. It is, of course,* SANDY *who buckles. She loves* MISS BRODIE, *wants her approval, so she sighs and tries to get it by giving* BRODIE *what she instinctively knows* BRODIE *wants.*)

SANDY. (*Sycophantically.*) I saw a picture of his

wife. She looked to me like a woman who wasn't going to have a prime. (BRODIE *smiles, pleased*.) There is a portrait he has done of his family. It starts with himself, very tall, then his wife. Then all the children graded downwards to the baby on the floor. It's a little bit amusing.

BRODIE. What makes it amusing?

SANDY. They all look like *you.*

BRODIE. Like me?

SANDY. Even the baby. Everybody he *paints* looks like *you.*

BRODIE. (*Strangely, mysteriously pleased, she smiles rather dreamily, speaks to* SANDY; *but as if she were not really conscious of the* GIRL'S *corporeal presence.*) Get out your putter, Sandy. We must attempt to correct your address. (*Her attention fades away; she is compelled to think and speak of* JENNY *and* LLOYD.) Does the painting of Jenny resemble me?

SANDY. Oh, yes.

BRODIE. Mr. Lloyd is bound to paint Jenny many times. She is the creme de la creme.

SANDY. (*Shrugs.*) He might want to paint me too.

BRODIE. (*Smiles patronizingly.*) I doubt if having your portrait painted is going to be your career, Sandy.

SANDY. (*Biting the bullet.*) What do *you* think it will be, Miss Brodie?

BRODIE. Your career?

SANDY. (*Ashamed, but unable to stop begging.*) Yes. What do you think it will be?

BRODIE. Well . . . you are quite intelligent, of course. (*Finally looks at* SANDY, *a long thoughtful gaze.*) This is the Twentieth Century. There are many outlets for an intelligent woman. (SANDY'S *tender young ego in total rout, she lets her hands go slack on the putter as she stares bitterly at her feet.*) Sandy, dear, you are not concentrating. (BRODIE *moves behind* SANDY, *puts her arms around the* GIRL, *guiding* SANDY'S *grip on the club.*) Thusly. Now try it. Again, but more slowly. Better. Better. Actually, Sandy, you have something more than mere intelligence.

You have got *insight*. Slowly, slowly. Again. *Much* better. (*Moves back the better to view* SANDY'S *corrected putting style. Takes a deep breath, smiles.*) You know, Sandy, it is on you and Jenny that I pin all my hopes. It is you and Jenny who are coming through. (SANDY *has begun to attend* BRODIE *closely, paying great attention to her every word and inflection.*) The fact is, *you* have got insight, though perhaps not quite spiritual, and *Jenny* has got instinct.

SANDY. (*Ducking her head and muttering as she uses the putter to swing.*) Though perhaps not quite spiritual . . .

BRODIE. What did you say?

SANDY. (*To distract* BRODIE.) Mr. Lowther has taken up golf, too.

BRODIE. Golf? (*Surprised.*) Mr. Lowther?

SANDY. For exercise, I expect. Mr. Lloyd said Mr. Lowther is putting on too much weight.

BRODIE. How do you know he has taken up golf?

SANDY. I saw him out playing with Miss Lockhart. Monica did too.

BRODIE. Miss Lockhart?

SANDY. The chemistry teacher.

BRODIE. Indeed. (*Shrugs.*) I know very little of Miss Lockhart. I leave her to her jars and gases. (*A moment of silence.*) We were talking about your insight, Sandy. *You* have insight, and Jenny has instinct. Jenny will be a great lover. The common moral code will not apply to her. She will be above it. This is a fact which only someone with insight should know about. Like you. (*Her voice lowers seductively.*) You, Sandy, *you* would make an excellent Secret Service agent. A great spy. (SANDY *turns, gives* BRODIE *one of her famous, small-eyed, searching looks.*) Really, Sandy. You must try not to peer at people. It gives a most rude impression.

SANDY. (*After a moment.*) Why do you think I would make a good spy?

BRODIE. Because you are intelligent . . . and not—*emotional.* I have observed this—constraint—in you. It has, from time to time, distressed me, as I, myself, am a *deeply* emotional woman. I feel many things passionately,

SANDY. (*Quietly.*) *I* feel things, Miss Brodie.

BRODIE. Everyone does, of course. It is a question of degree. (*Shrugs.*) Actually, *passion* would be a handicap to a spy. (*She has become aware of a rather long hiatus between choral selections.*) Oh, dear—can choir practice be over so soon? We shall have to cut our lesson short. Mr. Lowther will be down in a minute.

SANDY. Miss Brodie . . . what did you mean when you said Jenny was—above the common moral code?

BRODIE. Simply that it will not apply to her. She is the exception. And you and I can help Jenny to realize this.

SANDY. How?

BRODIE. Perhaps when she is eighteen—*soon*—she will *know love.*

SANDY. (*Solemnly.*) You mean she will have affairs. Love affairs.

BRODIE. Yes you *do!* You *do* have insight!

(BRODIE *and* SANDY *look deeply into one another's eyes; what either of them sees is, of course, imponderable. It is at this moment that* LOWTHER *comes running into the gymnasium. He is out of breath and appears to be highly agitated.*)

LOWTHER. Jean! Miss Mackay! Something ter— (SANDY's *presence stops him.*) something has come up!

BRODIE. What is it? What is the matter with you?

LOWTHER. (*Shakes his head nervously; is scarcely able to articulate his towering anxiety.*) *Miss Mackay!* She wants us in her study *immediately. Immediately!*

BRODIE. (*Instantly on her high horse.*) *I* am *not* accustomed to being summoned *immediately*—by anyone.

LOWTHER. (*Pleading.*) *Jean!* (*Made further frantic by the presence of* SANDY.) Miss *Brodie*—Sandy—uh—would you mind? Miss Brodie and I—we have some staff matters . . .

SANDY. (*Backing off.*) Oh—well—I have to get my books before class . . . Goodbye, Mr. Lowther. Goodbye, Miss Brodie . . . Thank you.

BRODIE. (*Casually.*) We will play a round at Braid Hills this weekend, Sandy. Just you and I. (BRODIE *stands immobile and silent until* SANDY *is out of sight.* LOWTHER *fidgets frantically. When* SANDY *is judged to be finally out of earshot.*) Really! Have you taken total leave of your senses, Gordon, to behave like that in front of a child!

LOWTHER. But, Jean, Miss Mackay—she's found something *incriminating!*

BRODIE. (*Raised eyebrows.*) What a melodramatic word, Gordon.

LOWTHER. Jean, I fear we are discovered! It's happened at last—we are ruined!

BRODIE. (*Distastefully.*) Ruined?

LOWTHER. (*Literally doing a little dance of anxiety.*) *Please.* She is *waiting.* She *dismissed my class*—and sent me to bring you to her! *Immediately.*

BRODIE. (*Gives him a look of icy disdain, then a little snort of cool laughter, shrugs.*) Very well, Gordon. *Anything* to calm *you.* Please make some attempt to pull yourself together. (*Strides off, leaving* LOWTHER *to stumble after her.*) I give you my word I won't let Miss Mackay stand you in the corner!

LIGHTS OUT

ACT TWO

SCENE 5

LIGHTS up on MACKAY'S *office.* MACKAY *faces* BRODIE *and* LOWTHER *from behind her desk. She is outwardly grim but within there beats a pulse that is pure pleasure, pure triumph.*

MACKAY. (*She waves a dirty, crumpled sheet of blue paper at* BRODIE.) *Now,* Miss Brodie. Do you know what this is?

BRODIE. It appears to be a scrap of paper.

MACKAY. It is, in fact, a *letter,* Miss Brodie. It was found by the gardener, concealed among the pots by the greenhouse. He glanced at it . . . He said after the first sentence he dared not actually *read* it. He brought it instantly to me.

BRODIE. (*All polite interest.*) Is it addressed to you?

MACKAY. No, Miss Brodie, it is addressed to Mr. Lowther. I propose to read it to you.

BRODIE. Should you, Miss Mackay? If it is addressed to Mr. Lowther—

MACKAY. (*Grimly.*) It is *signed by you,* Miss Brodie. Of course I realize it is a forgery. It is the work of a child . . . I shall begin.

BRODIE. Please do.

MACKAY. (*Gives her one last killing look, then begins to read.*) "My Dear Delightful Gordon, Your letter has moved me deeply as you may imagine. But alas, I must ever decline to be Mrs. Lowther. My reasons are twofold. I am dedicated to my girls as is Madame Pavlova, and there is another in my life. He is Teddy Lloyd! Intimacy has never taken place with him. He is married to another. We are not lovers, but we know the truth. However, I was proud of giving myself to you when you came and took me in the bracken while the storm raged about us. If I am in a certain condition—I shall place the infant in the care of a worthy shepherd and his wife. I may permit misconduct to occur again from time to time as an outlet because I am in my prime. We can also have many a breezy day in the fishing boat at sea. We must keep a sharp lookout, however, for Miss Mackay, as she is rather narrow which arises from an ignorance of culture and the Italian scene. I love to hear you singing 'Hey Johnnie Cope.' But were I to receive a proposal of marriage tomorrow from the Lord Lyon King of Arms I would decline it. Allow me in conclusion to congratulate you warmly on your sexual intercourse, as well as your singing. With fondest joy, Jean Brodie." (*As if handing over a box full of snakes,* MACKAY *leans across the desk and hands the letter to* BRODIE, *ignoring the shrunken* MR. LOWTHER.) Is this what your girls—your *"set"* has learned under your auspices, Miss Brodie?

BRODIE. (*Carefully, curiously, minutely, she goes over the letter. Finally she hands it back to* MACKAY.) A literary collaboration. There are two separate hands involved. One of the authors slants her tail consonants in an unorthodox manner, the other does not. Also, judging from the condition of the paper I should think it has been in the greenhouse quite a wee while.

MACKAY. Is that all you have to say?

BRODIE. What else is there to say? Two little girls at the age of budding sexual fantasy concoct a romance for themselves and choose me as a romantic symbol. Is that so surprising?

MACKAY. (*Aghast at* BRODIE's *aplomb.*) Do you deny that you encourage these fantasies, as you call them? Do you deny that by consorting openly with Mr. Lowther at Cramond you lead these poor children into the most— fevered conclusions? Not only Mr. Lowther but Mr. Lloyd is brought into the circle of fire! Mr. Lloyd, who has a wife and six children! It is diabolical! That infants should be knowledgeable of—

BRODIE. (*Reasonably.*) Eleven—twelve-year-old girls are not infants, Miss Mackay.

MACKAY. How do you know they are eleven—twelve?

BRODIE. From the handwriting—the vocabulary, and the very rudimentary knowledge of the facts of life. Surely you cannot believe that this is the work of nine-year-olds?

MACKAY. I could easily believe that it was the work of *your* nine-year-olds! (*Flips the paper over with distaste.*) In view of the age and condition of the paper . . . I will grant that it was probably composed— (*Shrugs.*) some time ago.

BRODIE. (*Mildly.*) Then I fail to understand your— agitation, Miss Mackay, over a rather *antique* prank.

MACKAY. (*Tight-lipped now indeed.*) Miss Brodie, there is a *principle* involved here. The principle that teachers are, prima facie, the protectors and guardians of their pupils. Guardians against *corruption*.

BRODIE. (*Calmly.*) But it is arguable, is it not, where guardianship ends and interference begins? When a girl reaches the age of twelve, one must accept that nature itself assumes the role of "corrupter."

MACKAY. One may accept, Miss Brodie, but one *need not stampede* the process. I submit, Miss Brodie, that your influence on your students has been both excessive and baneful.

(*After a moment as the* Two Women *stare at one another,* BRODIE *sighs, much put upon.*)

BRODIE. (*A rueful little laugh.*) There is very little for me to say, Miss Mackay, in the face of your extraordinary prejudice and hostility.

MACKAY. I am not asking you to say anything! I am asking—*demanding* that you put your signature— (*With heavy irony.*) your *own* signature—on a letter of resignation.

BRODIE. (*Her wrath finally beginning to crack the surface of her preternatural calm.*) I will not resign!

MACKAY. (*Utterly taken aback.*) You will not resign? You will force me to dismiss you?

BRODIE. I will not resign and you will not dismiss me, Miss Mackay. (*She rises to her full height. Sybil Thorndike would have applauded.*) I will not allow you to exercise on me your warped compulsion to persecute! I will not be slandered, hounded—you will *not* use the excuse of that pathetic—that *humorous* document to bully and blackmail me into resigning. Mr. Lowther—you are witness to this. Miss Mackay has made totally *unsupported* accusations against my good name. And yours. If she has one authentic shred of evidence, just *one*, let her bring it forth! Otherwise, if any further word of this outrageous calumny reaches my ears, I shall sue. I shall take Miss Mackay to the public courts, and I shall sue the trustees of Marcia Blaine School if they support her. I will not stand by and allow myself to be crucified by a woman whose *fetid* frustration has overcome her judgment! If scandal is to your taste, Miss Mackay, then I shall give you a *feast!*

MACKAY. (*Appalled.*) Miss Brodie!

BRODIE. I am a teacher! I am a teacher! First! Last! Always! Do you imagine for one instant that I will let that be taken from me without a fight? (*She is magnificent.* LOWTHER *can only admire her.* MACKAY *is stunned.*) I have dedicated, sacrificed my *life* to this profession. And I will not stand by like an inky little slacker and watch you rob me of it. And for *what* reason? *For jealousy.* Because I have the gift of claiming girls for my own. It is true that I am a strong influence on my girls. Yes! I am proud of it! I influence them to be aware of all the possibilities of life. Of Beauty, of Honor, of Courage. I do not, Miss Mackay, influence them to look for ugliness and slime where they *do not exist.* (*Takes a deep breath.*) My girls will be coming back from recreation so I shall return to my classroom. They will find me composed and prepared to reveal to them the succession of the Stuarts. (*Strides toward the door, turns.*) And on Sunday I shall visit Mr. Lowther at Cramond. We are accustomed, bachelor and spinster, to spend Sundays together in sailing, in walking the beaches, and in the pursuit of music. Mr. Lowther is teaching me the mandolin. Good day, Miss Mackay.

LIGHTS DIM OUT

CURTAIN

ACT TWO

SCENE 6

LIGHTS up quickly on BRODIE's *schoolroom. She strides nervily across to erase a board that does not need erasing. The door opens and* LOWTHER *enters, still carrying the golf clubs in his arms.*

LOWTHER. Oh, Jean! You were wonderful. Miss Mackay wants to make it up!

BRODIE. (*Grimly triumphant.*) I'm sure she does!

LOWTHER. You were heroic! Heroic! It was inspiring! Oh, if only I could have stood up like that to Mr. Gaunt! If I could have said, "*Mr.* Gaunt! If you have *one* authentic shred of evidence—just one—"

BRODIE. What are you talking about?

LOWTHER. Mr. Gaunt called on me the night before last. He advised me to resign as organist and elder of the church. He spoke very plainly.

BRODIE. (*Militantly.*) And what did you answer?

LOWTHER. (*Helplessly.*) He left me no alternative, Jean. I—resigned.

BRODIE. You *allowed* this evil-minded man—a man who uses his position as minister of the gospel to encourage the slanderous gossip of petty provincials—

LOWTHER. But Jean! It isn't just gossip! You do not go home on Sunday nights!

BRODIE. They have no proof! Can't you see that resignation is tantamount to a confession of guilt?

LOWTHER. (*With great feeling.*) I *feel* guilty!

BRODIE. Well, *I* do *not!*

LOWTHER. (*Sinks into one of the student's chairs,
drained, utterly fatigued.*) Oh, Jean . . . it's been going
on so *long.* Can't you see, I am not cut out to be a—
(*Ducks his head, whispers.*) a philanderer!

BRODIE. (*Throws back her head and laughs.*) A philanderer! Oh, Gordon!

LOWTHER. (*Stubbornly.*) Will you not marry me at
last and put an end to all this sneaking about?

BRODIE. (*Laughs.*) Only today I was told to my face
that you plan to marry the Chemistry teacher.

LOWTHER. (*Abashed.*) I played golf with Miss Lockhart once.

BRODIE. *Twice.*

LOWTHER. (*A paroxysm of shame.*) Twice.

BRODIE. Beware. Don't trifle with her. (*She points a
gun-like finger at his temple.*) She has the means to blow
us all up.

LOWTHER. Jean . . . Miss Lockhart means nothing to
me. You know that. It's just that so much of the time
now you are busy.

BRODIE. If you would only be persuaded to take a flat
in Edinburgh—

LOWTHER. I do not *want* a flat in Edinburgh. Cramond is my home! I was born there! You know I could
not leave Cramond. I don't *want* to leave Cramond.

BRODIE. You want a great deal, do you not?

LOWTHER. (*Contritely.*) What I want mostly, Jean, is
to see you happy and *safe.*

BRODIE. Safe? And what, pray, does safety have to do
with happiness? (*Laughs.*) I am not an admirer of
Stanley Baldwin. (*Suddenly fidgety and agitated.*) Oh,
do run along, Gordon. My class is almost due and I need
to compose myself.

LOWTHER. I don't understand you. You will not marry me and yet you feed me and share my bed.

BRODIE. Share your bed. Why can't you say you are my lover?

LOWTHER. I do not *want* to be your lover! I want to be your husband! And I'm sick and tired of all that rich, undomestic food. I want to go on my honeymoon to the Isle of Eigg near Rum where my mother and father went on their honeymoon, and I want to come back to Cramond with my bride! *That's* what I want! (*He stomps to the door, then turns.*) And I wanted to conduct the church choir, too! (*He is gone.*)

(LLOYD *enters.*)

LLOYD. I was nearly run down in the corridor by your young man . . . (*She does not answer.*) Rumors are flying . . . Did you get the sack?

BRODIE. (*Coolly.*) On the contrary. Miss Mackay experienced the utmost difficulty in persuading me to stay. *Utmost.* (*He gives a short laugh. Once again her eyes fix on him for a long moment. She breathes deeply.*) I hear you've been painting Jenny.

LLOYD. Yes.

BRODIE. (*Like a· blessing.*) I am glad. (*Something like a shudder passes over her and she turns away from him. During the next few speeches, she moves constantly from spot to spot, always as if to escape his eyes. She never looks at him directly.*) *Very* glad. Because . . . I've always sensed—sensed—

LLOYD. Sensed what?

BRODIE. Jenny's—potential. My own instincts are very strong—I felt this—this possibility—that Jenny could be magnificently elevated—above the ordinary run of lovers—

LLOYD. Of lovers?

BRODIE. She is getting more beautiful each year. She quite amazes me . . . I see her as becoming—Venus incarnate, something set apart— (*There is a rising note of something close to hysteria in her voice, an almost religious fervour.* LLOYD *is puzzled.*) You see it, don't you? You are an artist. You see things other men can't see. You *must* see it.

LLOYD. She is an uncommonly pretty girl.

BRODIE. No . . . No . . . it is much more than that . . . She has extraordinary physical instincts—primitive and free—

LLOYD. Primitive? Little *Jenny*? (*Smiles, but a trifle uncertainly.*) What are you up to, Jean?

BRODIE. Ah! (*She turns and faces him now.*) But the question is what are you up to, Mr. Lloyd? I'm only trying to tell you—that I understand—about Jenny. I've always known.

LLOYD. What the devil are you talking about? Known *what?*

BRODIE. (*Smiles, dreamily permissive.*) Why, that— that one day you would—paint Jenny. (*Her look is clearly one of sexual challenge.*)

LLOYD. (*He frowns, considering her, decides that she means precisely what he thinks she means. Flatly.*) Paint Jenny. (*He shakes his head and lets his breath out in a long, low whistle.*) Jean. It seems to me that you are *quite* aware of what you're doing.

BRODIE. What *I'm* doing?

LLOYD. You're trying to put that child in *my* bed. In *your* place.

BRODIE. (*Shivers, turns away from him.*) Don't be disgusting!

LLOYD. It's only the words that disgust you—you don't boggle at the *thought!* Do you? (*He pulls her roughly around to face him.*) Look at yourself! Look at what you're doing! Using little Jenny— (*Shakes his head with anger and frustration.*) and using old Lowther—making him play house—

BRODIE. I do not *use* Mr. Lowther! It is I who allow

myself to be used . . . I have devoted myself to Mr. Lowther! I give him every attention! Cook for him!

LLOYD. (*A burst of real laughter.*) Cook! You've stuffed him like a Strasbourg goose. Fed him in place of loving him, isn't that it?

BRODIE. (*Outraged.*) You know nothing about what there is of love between Gordon and me!

LLOYD. My God! All those boring hours in bed with old Lowther puffing bravely away— (*Her hand lashes out across his face. He steps in toward her, smiling.*) That's better, Jean. That's more like it. That was direct. That's the first actual contact between us in three years.

BRODIE. Get out! (*Gasping with dry sob.*) Get out of my class—my girls—

LLOYD. Your class! Your girls—your camouflage—your *cordon sanitaire!* (*The school BELL rings. He starts furiously toward the door, but pauses, looks back at her. When he speaks, his voice is calmer, his manner thoughtful.*) You know, Jean, you really ought to marry old Lowther. You really should. At least you'd have some protection. Don't you know that sooner or later Mackay will have your head on a platter?

BRODIE. (*Madly.*) I will prevail over Miss Mackay! I will prevail over the malice of this institution!

LLOYD. (*Tiredly.*) Over yourself, Jean. Just try to prevail over yourself.

(*He is interrupted by the entrance of the* CHILDREN, *who go to their desks, staring curiously at this* MAN *in whose presence their exciting* MISS BRODIE's *eyes flash and cheeks burn.*)

BRODIE. Girls— (*She takes a steadying breath.*) girls, this is Mr. Lloyd, the art master . . . When you graduate to the senior school—if he is still at Marcia Blaine— (*Her eyes challengingly on him.*) you will be fortunate enough to receive his artistic guidance—

LLOYD. Goodbye, girls. I'll see you in three years.

GIRLS. Goodbye, Mr. Lloyd.

LLOYD. Goodbye, Miss Brodie. I hope I will also see *you.*

BRODIE. (*Still trembling with rage and excitement, she turns to her* CLASS, *goes into her routine.*) We will *not* do our history today. Rather, I shall continue the story of my last holidays in Italy. I have brought you some pictures of Italy which I have placed upon the wall. Italy, where Mussolini has put an end to unemployment and there is no litter in the streets. I do not believe in talking down to children. (*She begins pointing out the pictures.*) Benito Mussolini, Italy's leader supreme. And here is a large formation of Il Duce's Fascisti. F-A-S-C-I-S-T-I. They are following him in a noble destiny. I myself mingled with such a crowd. I wore my silk dress with the red poppies which is right for my coloring. I saw again the Colosseum. The Colosseum where Christian slaves were thrown to lions and gladiators fought them to the death. (*Head bravely up, her arm raised, in the gladiator's salute.*) "Ave imperator! Morituri te salutamus!" "Hail Caesar! We who are about to die, salute thee!" (*The* LITTLE GIRLS *thrill and gasp.*) Florence. The David of Michelangelo . . . He stands in Florence in the Piazza del Popolo for any passerby to gaze upon. He is at once the glory of the past and the inspiration of the future. David the Young Warrior. (*The rest of the soliloquy delivered with ever-mounting tension, as* BRODIE's *violently stimulated imagination runs over wild and dangerous track, far from the class of small girls in her charge.*) There is a famous picture of Dante meeting Beatrice . . . It is pronounced Beatrichay in Italian, which makes it very beautiful. Meeting Beatrichay on the Ponte Vecchio— the Old Bridge—he fell in love with her at that moment. He was a man in his middle years, she was fourteen—that can happen. A mature man can find love in a young girl, a very young girl—find the spring and essence of all old loves. It is not unlikely, though we shall never know, that Beatrichay reminded Dante sharply in that moment on the Ponte Vecchio of an old love, a lost love—a *sublime* love—and he was seized with such a longing— (*A shudder, a gasp for breath, an effort to force open heavy lids.*) That picture—that picture was painted by Rossetti. Who was Dante Gabriel Rossetti? Who was *Dante Gabriel Rossetti?*

CLARA. (*Frightened and excited in turn,* CLARA *manages to whisper the answer.*) A painter, Miss Brodie.

BRODIE. Yes! A painter . . . A painter . . .

LIGHTS DIM SLOWLY

ACT THREE

Scene 1

The Convent. HELENA *and* MR. PERRY *as before.*

MR. PERRY. All I meant was that a child acting on a child's distorted view can be dangerous.

HELENA. But I do not believe that the views of the young are, inevitably, distorted. On the contrary, I believe that the observations of children are remarkably truthful.

MR. PERRY. But what a dangerous and tentative truth. Because observation is only the first step toward judgement. Somewhere in between must come the one quality that children seldom possess.

HELENA. Indeed? Then perhaps you will instruct me.

MR. PERRY. (*Aware that he is being baited, smiles cautiously.*) You are asking an American Baptist to instruct *you*, Sister Helena?

HELENA. I am vowed to the practice of humility, Mr. Perry.

MR. PERRY. (*It is touché. He grins acknowledgement.*) Then I would say that one's ability to see truthfully is conditioned by one's willingness to see—charitably. And the young are too arbitrary to be charitable. Am I tiring you, Sister?

HELENA. No. (*A sigh.*) Perhaps you are right. (*Smiles.*) At one point Miss Brodie was judged to be a Fascist.

MR. PERRY. Oh?

HELENA. When I entered the Catholic Church, I found in its ranks quite a number of Fascists much less agreeable than Miss Brodie.

MR. PERRY. I assume you mean that humorously, Sister.

HELENA. Oh, no. I have no humor. Irony, perhaps, but

no humor. Nor had Miss Brodie. Humor would have helped Miss Brodie. It might have extended her prime.

MR. PERRY. Why? Was it cut short?

HELENA. Yes. It had to be.

MR. PERRY. What happened?

HELENA. Miss Brodie was . . . assassinated . . .

BLACKOUT

ACT THREE

SCENE 2

It is two and a half years later.

LLOYD'S *studio. Posed, her back to us, is a* GIRL, *obviously naked except for a towel wrapped turban-like around her head. She seems to be reading, occasionally turning pages. Beyond his* MODEL, *facing her and us, is* LLOYD. *He is at his easel, painting.*

LLOYD. Where you are mistaken is in supposing that Jean Brodie is unique . . . (*The* GIRL *seems to pay him no mind, continues to read.*) There is an army of these ladies in Edinburgh—war-bereaved spinsters—studying German—living on nuts and honey . . . It is simply that they do not attempt, like Jean, to teach in schools of traditional character. (*He moves from the easel toward his* MODEL, *bending to correct a fold in the turban. He circles her, his eyes pleased with her.*) Jean is a magnificent specimen.

SANDY. She's crackers!

LLOYD. How graciously you put it.

SANDY. And if she knew I were sitting for you instead of Jenny, they would have to take her away in a net.

LLOYD. In a net!

SANDY. I think I'll start a whispering campaign.

LLOYD. Why should you want to hurt her?

(*Her head moves to follow* LLOYD, *we see her profile. It is* SANDY.)

SANDY. You have instinct, Teddy, but no insight. She's not magnificent. She's a ridiculous woman!

LLOYD. There is no contradiction in being both ridiculous and magnificent. Your young mind will have to stretch a bit to grasp that.

SANDY. I think my mind has stretched astonishingly to be able to discuss, at *sixteen* . . . the enduring passion of my lover for another woman.

LLOYD. It is not only astonishing, Sandy, it is unnatural. You are far too analytical for your age. At your age you should be passionate and involved and short-sighted.

SANDY. Why? Because your ideal is? At forty—whatever—she is? Her and her passions! She's got a new one this term. You should see her skulking around trying to raise funds for Franco!

LLOYD. (*Laughs.*) Oh, my God. Franco!

SANDY. Yes, we've gone very Spanish this season—what with the war and Mary MacGregor's brother.

LLOYD. What? That chap who's so careless with his tutors? What about him?

SANDY. Didn't you know? He's run off to Spain. To fight. Miss Brodie is beside herself. (*They freeze in position. LIGHTS fade on them.*)

(*LIGHTS up on school lawn.* BRODIE *is surrounded by* YOUNG GIRLS, *her new class.*)

BRODIE. Little girls, you must all grow up to be dedicated women as I have dedicated myself to you. Dedication is the order of the day. In Germany there is Hitler, a prophet-like figure like Thomas Carlyle. Perhaps more reliable than the essentially Latin Mussolini . . . (MARY *joins the* GROUP.) And in Spain there is, of course, Gen-eralissimo Franco. *El Jefe. The Chief. (Notices* MARY.) Ah! Here is our Mary! (*The* LITTLE GIRLS *eye* MARY *reverently*.) Has there been any word from your brother, Mary dear?

MARY. No, Miss Brodie. N—nothing. But Mr. Ealing at the b—bank is s—sending men from the Foreign Office —to Spain!

BRODIE. Your brother is being sent for? *Sent for?* (*Laughs harshly*.) Mr. Ealing at the bank would *send* for Caesar! Would *send* to fetch Richard Coeur de Lion home from the Crusades! Mr. Ealing at the bank has tried throughout history to stay the march of civilization. But Franco's Army comprises all the best elements of Spain and their supporters, banded together to protect their property and their religion . . . (*Hesitates, frowns*.) regrettably Roman Catholic. Nevertheless, they are com-mitted to God rather than to the powers of chaos and anarchy—committed to heroic action. All you little girls are living in a time that will demand all you have to give of courage and gallantry. You must remember that it was for *you* that Hugh fell. It was for you that a great and terrible war was fought. It was for you that a new world was begun. You must become *heroines* to live in this new world. Heroines!

LITTLE GIRL. Do you mean that we will have to march—

SECOND GIRL. —and shoot *guns?*

BRODIE. (*Fiercely*.) If you are called!

THIRD GIRL. Girls?

BRODIE. Have you never heard of Hanna Snell? An English girl who sailed with Boscowan's fleet and fought at Araapong. She was wounded, but without medical help she extracted a bullet from her own shoulder and lived to serve again! Hanna Snell was a *girl!*

MARY. (*Thrilled*.) Oh!

BRODIE. (*To all the* GIRLS.) You too must be prepared

to serve, suffer, and sacrifice. Are you prepared? (*Eyes them fiercely.*)

GIRLS. (*Mesmerized.*) Yes, Miss Brodie!

BRODIE. (*Solemnly.*) Dismissed! (*The* GIRLS *disperse. A few solemn "Goodbye, Miss Brodie," one or two "Goodbye, Mary," then* BRODIE *and* MARY *are alone: Possessively.*) Well, Mary MacGregor. We have a great deal to discuss, have we not? This proposed fetching home of your brother is outrageous. You and I, Mary dear, *you* and *I* must find some way to do our own good part . . .

(*The LIGHTS darken on the school lawn and then come back up on Lloyd's studio.*)

LLOYD. Jean knows nothing of politics nor politicians. She simply invests all leaders with her own romantic vision.

SANDY. I'm tired.

LLOYD. Take a break. I'll pour you a cup of tea.

SANDY. Do you know it occurs to me that the Brodie Set has been Miss Brodie's faithful Fascisti—F-A-S-C-I-S-T-I—and that accounts for her disapproval of the Girl Guides. The Guides are a rival Fascisti, and she cannot bear it. (*Laughs.*) How I wish I'd joined the Brownies.

LLOYD. What a spiteful child it is.

SANDY. I'm ashamed I ever loved Miss Brodie.

LLOYD. Never regret having loved anyone, Sandy.

SANDY. (*Suddenly a child again.*) But . . . Miss Brodie never loved *me*.

LLOYD. (*Smiles.*) How can you know that?

SANDY. She only—*uses* people.

LLOYD. We all do that. What else is there for us to use —the people we love—the people who love us?

SANDY. Oh, don't try to be philosophical with *me*, Teddy. You have a perfectly good mind, but you refuse to use it.

LLOYD. And you, my love, have a perfectly good heart —but you're too young to trust it.

SANDY. Ah! My age does bother you, doesn't it? (*Picks up her book.*) You should read Freud—it's very enlightening.

LLOYD. My dear, I live in terror of further enlightenment. (*Takes volume of Freud away from her. Nods, indicating book.*) But you are quite right about your mind having been stretched. What needs a wee bit o' stretchin', lass, is your immortal soul. (*Picks up a book of his own.*) Try this for size. If you're so clever, perhaps you will be able to explain it to me. I've been reading and puzzling over it for twenty years.

SANDY. Saint Augustine . . . *The City of God.* (*Grins at him—mocking.*) A rival prophet?

LLOYD. A rival *teacher.* Clever fellow. Do you know what he said? He said, "Give me chastity and give me continency, but do not give it yet."

SANDY. (*Laughs.*) Very much your sort of teacher, I'd say. (*Teasingly presents a bare shoulder to vamp him.*) How much longer will you be tempted by this firm, young flesh?

LLOYD. (*Embraces her casually.*) Till you're eighteen and over the hill. (*He kisses her lightly, and before anything can develop, she pulls away.*)

SANDY. Take me dancing.

LLOYD. Certainly not.

SANDY. What a coward.

LLOYD. A man with a wife and a large family plus a schoolgirl for a mistress can be called any number of rude names. But "coward" is not one of them.

SANDY. Well, if you won't take me dancing, take me to church.

LLOYD. Take yourself to church. (*Puts his face against her neck.*) So sweet—the flesh of the neck. If only this could be bottled and sold across the counter! Little girl . . . schoolgirl . . . devil . . .

SANDY. (*Laughs softly.*) I really shouldn't feed your depraved appetites . . . (*Kisses him.*) Lloyd . . . Lloyd . . . (*Pulls at his hair.*) when can I see the portrait?

LLOYD. Never. I shall never finish it . . . We will simply go on like this until one or both of us is dead—

SANDY. (*Abruptly pulls away from him and stands up.*) No. *Now.* (*Teasing.*) I want to see myself mirrored in your eyes. I need a vision of myself.

(*He attempts to grab her arm, but she evades him and goes to the easel on which rests the work in progress.*)

LLOYD. No! No. Sandy—it's not ready—I am not pleased with it yet—

SANDY. (*Fondly.*) Oh, you. You'll never be pleased. (*Before he can get to her, she pulls the cloth from the painting.*)

LLOYD. (*In despair.*) No Sandy—wait! (*She stares at the picture for a long while, wordless, expressionless. LLOYD pleads.*) I cannot help myself, Sandy. Believe me —it has nothing to do with what I feel for you.

SANDY. (*Calmly.*) Even the skin tones are hers. It is not even my skin. I never really believed you loved me . . . But I thought—I really thought that you— (*Shrugs, attempts a smile.*) *desired* me. Desired *me*.

LLOYD. I *did*—I mean I *do!*

SANDY. It might just as well have been Jenny after all. It would be the same with anyone. Well, Lloyd. I congratulate you on the economy of your style. Simply use whatever is at hand. (*Laughs in genuine amusement.*) Miss Brodie does it too. I used to be fascinated by the variations of her Hugh-who-fell-in-Flanders-Field love story . . . First she would give him the talents of the art master, and then those of the singing master. How similar your techniques are! Very instructive! (*Grabs up her clothes and begins to dress.*)

LLOYD. (*Pleading.*) Sandy, love is the most irrational thing on God's earth. Do you think I *choose* to love Jean Brodie? If I could choose, I would love my wife—or *you.* You are the most remarkable girl I have ever known. You are astonishing and marvelous and *desirable*. Why would I not choose you if I could choose? Don't think less of yourself because I am bewitched.

SANDY. Very well. I shan't.

LLOYD. Believe what I am telling you.

SANDY. I believe you. I even believe you are bewitched. I am not sure about God, but I am now *quite* sure about witches. (*She resumes dressing. This time with more purpose.*)

LLOYD. Where are you going? Sleep here. Say you are at Jenny's—to study. I will stay with you. I can tell Dierdre I fell asleep. I have before.

SANDY. (*She shakes her head.*) That's very kind of you, Teddy. I know you don't like to worry Dierdre.

LLOYD. (*Puzzled and intimidated by her poise.*) Will you be back tomorrow?

SANDY. Oh, no. I won't be back. It would really be a waste of time, wouldn't it?

LLOYD. I can't bear to hear you speak so bitterly.

SANDY. (*Seriously.*) I don't think I'm bitter. I think what I am is . . . *interested*. I may take the *City of God*, mayn't I?

LLOYD. Of course.

SANDY. Good night, Teddy. (*She starts for the door, opens it, turns, smiling, nods toward the picture.*) You can go on painting. You don't really need a model. (*She pauses. He turns to her. She gives him a dazzling, but small-eyed smile.*) Since this seems to be a time for truth . . . you are quite a mediocre painter, Teddy. You'll never be really good. I wonder you don't try some other line. You are getting along, you know. (*Once again she is gone.*)

LIGHTS DOWN QUICKLY

ACT THREE

SCENE 3

Lights on SANDY, MONICA, *and* JENNY. MONICA *is very excited.*

JENNY. Are you certain?

MONICA. (*Dramatically insistent to* SANDY.) Of course I'm certain! They've been trying to find her for three days!

JENNY. But what would *Mary* go to *Spain* for? I thought she was home with the flu!

MONICA. That's just what they put out when she disappeared. But she left a note saying she was going to Spain to join her brother to fight for Franco.

JENNY. To *fight!* But she could get *shot!*

SANDY. "Without medical help she would extract the bullet from her own shoulder and live to serve again!"

(JENNY *giggles, but* MONICA *is indignant.*)

MONICA. It isn't funny! She could really get hurt! She could get killed!

(*Enter* LLOYD. *He has approached the* GROUP *from behind* SANDY. *She is not aware of him until he speaks.*)

LLOYD. What's going on? Who could get killed?

(SANDY *edges to one side, as if to avoid any possible physical contact with* LLOYD. *But she returns his gaze unflinchingly.*)

MONICA. Mary MacGregor! She's run away to Spain to fight!

LLOYD. (*Totally disbelieving.*) *Mary MacGregor?* What kind of joke is this?

JENNY. It isn't a joke! She's really gone! To *Spain!* It's true! They're been trying to find her for days!

LLOYD. (*Grins.*) Mary MacGregor couldn't negotiate her way across Edinburgh.

MONICA. (*Shakes her head furiously.*) No! They've traced her all the way to the Spanish border!

LLOYD. I don't believe it. She'd never make it on her own.

SANDY. (*Quietly.*) Oh, I don't expect she was on her own. She has a—guiding spirit.

LLOYD. What are you talking about?

SANDY. I'm sure Miss Brodie gave Mary very explicit directions. 'The Paris train will take you as far as Perpignan, Mary. P-e-r-p-i-g-n-a-n. Now—pounds are in this envelope and francs are in this envelope and pesos are in *this* envelope . . .' (*They* ALL *stare at* SANDY. *She shrugs.*) How else?

LLOYD. (*He frowns furiously, trying not to believe.*) I don't believe it. (*But, of course, he does.*)

MONICA. Nor do I.

JENNY. Nor do I.

MONICA. Miss Brodie will be frantic!

SANDY. Miss Brodie will be *ecstatic.*

MONICA. (*Becoming quite hostile to* SANDY.) Come on, *Jenny.* I want to go and talk to *Miss Brodie.* (*The* TWO GIRLS *exit.* SANDY *turns, starts off alone in the opposite direction.*)

LLOYD. (*He is nervous, uneasy.*) Sandy . . . do you really believe what you said? That Jean sent that child off to Spain?

SANDY. How can you doubt it? (*She turns on her heel, exits, leaving* LLOYD *to stand, distracted, worried, alone as:*)

THE LIGHTS DIM

ACT THREE

Scene 4

Late afternoon a day later. The classroom. A large map of Spain is pinned to the blackboard. Brodie *is marking map.* Lloyd *enters.*

Lloyd. Moving your troops to Barcelona? Well, Jean, I hear you've been raising funds for Franco.

Brodie. Yes.

Lloyd. You must have—inspired Mary MacGregor.

Brodie. She went to join her brother—he is her only kin.

Lloyd. (*Shrugs.*) I find it extraordinary.

Brodie. The *times* are extraordinary!

Lloyd. (*He makes his decision. Takes a deep breath, plunges.*) Well. I too am attempting to raise funds. For a worthy cause. (*Smiles.*)

Brodie. (*Pleased.*) A cause? *You?* What sort of cause?

Lloyd. (*He takes his time answering. When he finally does speak, the words pour out as if they had been rehearsed.*) A romantic one. I'm taking up a collection to buy a wedding present for Mr. Lowther and Miss Lockhart. . . . May I put you down for one pound? (*Hands her small notebook.*) It's to be a simple affair at Cramond Kirk a week on Sunday. The young lovers announced their intention to Miss Mackay evening before last. Her delight was so profound that she ran amok and toasted them in neat whisky.

Brodie. (*A moment of stunned silence, then tremblingly.*) And who told you to come to me with this? *Who?*

Lloyd. (*Quietly.*) I volunteered. I, said the sparrow, with my bow and arrow, I volunteered.

Brodie. (*Her anger rising to save her.*) And what kill, pray, did you expect to make? Do you think I could not with one snap of my fingers send poor Miss Lockhart back to her gaseous domain? It was *I* who prevailed upon Mr. Lowther to take this step. It was I who encouraged him in his reluctant pursuit of Miss Lockhart. No. What I cannot understand is *you*. I cannot understand your malice in coming to me in this way, hoping to hurt and humiliate me. *Why?*

LLOYD. I don't know. It's true. It's what I wanted. To hurt you.

BRODIE. Why are you so angry with me? Why?

LLOYD. I'm frightened. I have a large family dependent on me. . . . I need my job at Marcia Blaine. I think I've owed a great deal more to old Lowther than I've ever cared to admit. I don't feel safe with you at large. It would seem there's something to be said for Stanley Baldwin after all. I'm forty-three years old, Jean. How old are you?

BRODIE. I'm in my prime!

LLOYD. Your prime forsooth! Look at yourself! Look at *me*. A third-rate artist—a small time womanizer running to seed. You're not in your prime, Jean—you're a frustrated spinster taking it out in idiot causes and dangerous ideas—a cranky schoolmarm—

BRODIE. I am a *teacher!*

LLOYD. A teacher or a leader? "A prophet-like figure"? The dangerous Miss Brodie and her troops! (*Now quietly.*) Well, where you lead, I cannot follow. I'm sorry, Jean. Goodbye. (*He is gone.*)

BRODIE. (*When she is sure that he is out of the room, she turns around toward the door, smiles tremulously; her fingers touch her lips in the gesture of a thrown kiss; she whispers:*) Arivederci . . .

LIGHTS OUT

ACT THREE

SCENE 5

*The classroom three days later. The LIGHTS come up
very slowly on a large group of* GIRLS, *little ones
and big ones together. They are standing, facing*
BRODIE, *who addresses them quietly.*

BRODIE. Girls, I have called you together, my special
girls, to tell you the truth about Mary MacGregor's death.
Miss Mackay has already announced the facts of Mary's
death in Spain but only I can tell you the truth. Mary
MacGregor died a heroine. It was her intention to fight
for Franco against the powers of darkness . . . So although the train that she was in was bombed before she
herself could strike a blow, her intention was a noble and
heroic one . . . (*The LIGHTS up full now as* BRODIE
speaks to the GIRLS; *her tears are in check, her voice is
sweet, exalted.*) Had she lived, Mary MacGregor would
have become a woman of great spirit and initiative . . .
Hers would have been a dedicated life . . . You must all
grow up to be dedicated women as Mary MacGregor dedicated her youth to a cause—as I have dedicated myself to
you. Tonight, little girls, let your imaginations soar. Think
on Joan of Arc, think on Florence Nightingale, think on
Mary MacGregor. Who amongst *you* has the makings of
a heroine? (*A hand is raised.*) Yes, Clara?

CLARA. May we think on *you*, Miss Brodie?

BRODIE. (*Doesn't smile, accepts the tribute seriously
and sadly.*) Well, why not? Deep in most of us is a
potential for greatness. Or the potential to inspire greatness. The day draws late. Your families will be expecting
you. Take home the story of Mary MacGregor

(*The* CHILDREN *move quietly out, saying subdued good-
byes to* BRODIE *as they empty from the room.*
JENNY, MONICA *and* SANDY *are left.*)

JENNY. Miss Brodie, I thought—*we* thought you might like us to stay with you for the rest of the day.

BRODIE. Oh, Jenny, you are considerate, but—I think I'd like to be alone for a while. (JENNY *nods, gently reaches out and touches* BRODIE'S *hand, leaves the room, followed by* MONICA *who is silently sobbing.* SANDY *moves to follow them, but is stopped by* BRODIE, *who detains her in silence until she is sure the* OTHER GIRLS *are out of hearing.*) I—I thought that *you* and *I* might go home to tea . . . You are my private ear, Sandy, my spiritual confidante. I can't think what I should do without you.

SANDY. I'm sorry, but I have some work to do.

BRODIE. (*Sighs.*) I want to talk to you, Sandy, about Mary.

SANDY. I'm sorry, Miss Brodie.

BRODIE. (*Fondly.*) How busy and grown-up you have become . . . But you mustn't forget, Sandy—how very much I *depend* on you. (SANDY *doesn't answer.*) Well, I won't try to keep you. (*Smiles.*) A toute a l'heure, Sandy, dear. (SANDY *is almost out the door when* BRODIE *calls out.* SANDY *looks back inquiringly.*) Sandy! It is on you and Jenny that I pin all my hopes.

(SANDY *gazes at her; then, without speaking, exits. LIGHTS come down on the classroom as we follow* SANDY. *She walks slowly, thoughtfully, finally enters the locker room. There she stands for a moment, making no move to unburden herself of books. At last there is the sound of someone approaching. Instinctively,* SANDY *steps behind a locker.* MACKAY *enters. Moves purposefully across the room, then stops, conscious of the other presence. She turns, peers about to see who is there.*)

MACKAY. Sandy? My word, you startled me. What are you doing still here? I was about to lock up. (*She sighs, seems to feel the need to talk, as much to herself as to* SANDY.) What a day this has been. Everything at sixes and sevens. (*Heavily.*) *Mary MacGregor.* I simply don't know what to think about what she did. It was so—*bizarre.* Poor child. I think she must have been very lonely. (*Gazes curiously at* SANDY.) But then, of course, she had the "set" as it were . . . You are all so close. Dear Miss Brodie—a remarkable woman, of course—a vigorous teacher. I have sometimes thought her talents a trifle *too* vigorous. For such *young* children. (*A pause. When nothing is forthcoming from* SANDY, *she sighs, continues. A rueful smile is offered* SANDY.) Ah well, "What canna be cured maun be endured." Don't think I'm *criticising* Miss Brodie. Though she likes her wee drink, I expect.

SANDY. (*Quietly.*) She doesn't drink, except a sherry on her birthday. Half a bottle between the five of us.

MACKAY. (*She is accustomed to defeat.*) That's all I meant, of course.

SANDY. (*A brief moment, and then, the plunge.*) You won't be able to pin her down on drink or sex. She's too careful. Have you thought of politics?

MACKAY. What did you say?

SANDY. I said, have you thought of politics?

MACKAY. I didn't know Miss Brodie was attracted by politics.

SANDY. Neither is she, except as a side interest. An attitude. She's simply a born Fascist. Have you thought of that?

MACKAY. (*Gives the* GIRL *a piercing stare, then turns, moves off, her face showing surprise, but also the willingness to accept and use this latest possible weapon against her old enemy. Abruptly, she begins to walk faster. Without looking back at* SANDY, *she issues a brief, but utterly commanding:*) Come to my study.

(MACKAY *exits.* SANDY *hesitates, then slowly, but steadily,* SANDY *follows* MACKAY *off.*)

LIGHTS DOWN SLOWLY

ACT THREE

SCENE 6

A few days later. MACKAY'S *office.* MACKAY *and* BRODIE *are standing across from one another.*

MACKAY. And it is the Board of Governors' decision that you will leave the school today. (*With great authority, quietly but utterly steadfast.*) If you prefer, you can leave directly from this office and I will have your belongings sent to you. (*For the first time since we have known her, some of the wind is really taken out of* BRODIE. *She rises slowly, but makes no attempt to go. She just stands, staring at* MACKAY. *She is winded, but not yet defeated.* MACKAY *eyes her, then makes a decision, speaks again.*) Miss Brodie, I have seriously considered whether I ought to tell you this . . . I think now perhaps I should. It was one of your own girls—your "set"—who put the enquiry in motion. So you see, Miss Brodie, this judgment against you is rather—far-reaching. I beg you to consider this—when you do finally stop to examine your conscience. (*Steps quietly to the door, holds it open.*) Goodbye, Miss Brodie. (*Like a sleepwalker,* MISS BRODIE *turns, walks blindly past* MACKAY *and out the door.*) Goodbye. (BRODIE *stops, turns her face back towards her tormentor.* MACKAY *speaks with some faintly revealed sense of pain and embarrassment for* BRODIE.) I'm sure you've been informed of the little celebration this afternoon in the staff room honoring Mr. Lowther and Miss Lockhart. I shall make your apologies —if you like.

(BRODIE *nods, walks on.* MACKAY *watches after her for a moment, then sighs deeply, closes her door. The LIGHTS spot* BRODIE'S *slow, shatteringly silent exit from Mackay's office.*)

BLACKOUT

ACT THREE

SCENE 7

LIGHTS up. SANDY'S bedroom. She is in a wrapper, lying on her bed, reading. It is the St. Augustine. A KNOCK. SANDY frowns, looks up.

SANDY. Yes?

(BRODIE *enters.* SANDY *regards* BRODIE *with such a stillness, such a shrinking silence that it seems almost to be horror.*)

BRODIE. Your mother told me to come in. She says you have not been feeling well . . . (*Still* SANDY *doesn't speak.*) that you've been away from school all week . . . (*A touch of the old crispness.*) Not that missing class is of any great concern. In my experience clever scholars are all too often *retarded* by dull and unimaginative teachers. (SANDY *still does not speak, and* BRODIE *too falls silent. Distractedly,* BRODIE *looks unseeing about the room. When she finally speaks again, her voice is tremulous and bewildered.*) Sandy . . . I believe I am—past my prime. (SANDY *doesn't speak.*) I had reckoned on my prime lasting until I was—at least fifty . . . Are you listening, Sandy?

SANDY. (*Whispers.*) Yes, Miss Brodie.

BRODIE. I have been dismissed from Marcia Blaine. I have been accused of teaching treason and sedition to my students. (*A short laugh, a faint note of hysteria in it.*) I am being transported for radicalism—like Thomas Muir of Hunter's Hill. (*Again a short pause as if she needs these short periods to draw upon almost depleted strength.*) Sandy . . . I had to see you. Sandy . . . you will not believe this, but Miss Mackay stated flatly that it is one of my own set who betrayed me. It is Monica, of course. (*Stares at* SANDY *for the shock she needs to see. If possible there is even less expression on* SANDY'S *face.*

But her hands begin to tremble slightly, causing the book she is still holding to shake. Quickly, she lays it down. BRODIE *seems not to notice this, staring only at* SANDY'S *face.*) I see you are not surprised. There is very little soul behind all of Monica's easy emotion.

SANDY. (*Terribly distressed.*) Monica is a loyal girl.

BRODIE. (*Bitterly.*) She *betrayed* me. I renounced the man I love! I gave up Teddy Lloyd to *consecrate* my life to you girls. To you and Jenny and Monica. Why did Monica do it?

SANDY. Miss Brodie . . . you mustn't . . . blame Monica . . .

BRODIE. Jenny. There is, at least, Jenny. She and Mr. Lloyd will soon be lovers. Perhaps with Jenny . . . she will encourage him. Mr. Lloyd will give up teaching and prepare an exhibition. Jenny will know, through *me*, how to help him. I have that. (*Blinks at* SANDY *as if suddenly reminded of her existence.*)

SANDY. (*During* BRODIE'S *speech about* JENNY *and* LLOYD, *some life, some raging hurt, has revived in* SANDY. *And at last, when* BRODIE *again carelessly lays claim to* SANDY'S *loyalty, the* GIRL *stiffens.*) Do you think you are Providence? That you can—can ordain love?

BRODIE. (*Dimly.*) What?

SANDY. (*Flatly.*) You haven't pulled it off. Jenny will not be Teddy Lloyd's lover.

BRODIE. (*Impatiently.*) What are you saying, Sandy?

SANDY. Jenny will not be Teddy's lover and I will not be your spy—your "Secret Service."

BRODIE. (*Utterly disoriented.*) My spy? What on earth are you talking about? *I have been dismissed from Marcia Blaine!* Why are you sitting there talking about Providence and the Secret Service? What is the matter with you? Are you running a *fever?*

SANDY. No. Not a fever.

BRODIE. Then *whatever* are you talking about?

SANDY. (*Frightened, but with determination.*) I am Teddy's lover.

BRODIE. What?

SANDY. I am Teddy's lover. Is that so difficult to believe? What does it matter to you which one of us it is? It doesn't matter to Teddy.

BRODIE. (*Stares at her.*) You are Teddy's lover?

SANDY. Yes.

BRODIE. (*Suddenly goes prim in a very Scottish way.*) Whatever possessed you! He is a Roman Catholic! How could a girl with a mind of her own, a girl with insight— have to do with a man who can't think for himself!

SANDY. (*For the first time, a faint smile creases* SANDY's *face.*) That doesn't seem to have bothered either of us, does it? We were neither of us very interested in his mind.

BRODIE. How dare you speak to me in this manner? (*Vaguely.*) I don't understand. I don't seem . . . to understand . . . what has happened . . . to everyone . . . Where has everyone *gone?*

SANDY. (*The Pope.*) Only *Mary* is gone.

BRODIE. What has Mary got to do with—

SANDY. Miss Brodie—*Mary MacGregor* is *dead.*

BRODIE. (BRODIE *blinks at her, unable to follow the jumps.*) Oh, poor Mary—

SANDY. Are you aware of the order of importance in which you place your—anxieties? One, you have been "betrayed"; two, who is or is not to be your proxy in Teddy Lloyd's bed; three, Mary's death! Miss Brodie, aren't you concerned at *all* with Mary's death?

BRODIE. I *grieve* for Mary!

SANDY. It was because of *you* she went.

BRODIE. Because of *me?* It was her *brother!* The poor unfortunate girl hadn't anyone else in the world.

SANDY. *No.* She had *you. That* was her misfortune. To please you, that silly stupid girl ran off and placed herself under a bomb! And you don't feel *responsible* for that?

BRODIE. No! No! I feel responsible for giving her ideals! The ideals that sent her to Spain, yes! By the way she died Mary MacGregor illumined her life! She died a heroine!

SANDY. She died a *fool!* Joining her brother to fight for Franco! Wasn't that just like Mary? Her brother is fighting for the other side! Her brother is fighting for the Republicans! Mary was headed for the *wrong army!*

BRODIE. (*Dazed, almost as if she were once again reprimanding* MARY.) Mary MacGregor.

SANDY. Mary *MacGregor* . . . I used to wonder why you always called Mary by her full name. I think it was because you had a hard time remembering who she *was.* Poor dim Mary—

BRODIE. I was devoted to Mary!

SANDY. No . . . She only appealed to your vanity.

BRODIE. (*Stares at her.*) What has happened? Why have you turned against me? You most of all? What have I done to you?

SANDY. (*She is not at all sure just what it is that* BRODIE *has done to* her. *This confusion causes her to shrug and speak with sullen reproach.*) You aren't good for people.

BRODIE. In what way? In what way, Sandy, was I not good for *you?*

SANDY. You are unwholesome and dangerous and children should not be exposed to you!

BRODIE. (*Cries out.*) How can you think it? How can you think I would harm you?

SANDY. But you *have.* You *have* harmed me!

BRODIE. *How?*

SANDY. (*As she is totally uncertain in her mind as to just* how *she has been harmed, she must return to her principal rationale for what she has done.*) You have *murdered* Mary!

BRODIE. It is you who betrayed me.

SANDY. No, I simply put a stop to you, Miss Brodie.

BRODIE. You have assassinated *me!*

SANDY. (*The accusation touches a nerve, and* SANDY *reacts furiously.*) Why must you always strike attitudes?

You really are a *ridiculous* woman! (BRODIE *seems quite literally to shrink under this last, mortal blow. Watching her,* SANDY, *too, seems to become physically diminished, once again frightened, not by* BRODIE, *but by her own triumph over the older woman.* SANDY *turns away from the sight. As* BRODIE *continues silent,* SANDY *finally speaks, her voice young, uncertain.*) Well—what will you do? *Now.*

BRODIE. Do? I—I don't know . . . (*Desperately pulling the tattered remnants of her old asperity about her, showing her power, perhaps for the final time.*) But . . . I am a descendant, do *not forget,* of Willie Brodie! He was a man of substance, a cabinet-maker and a designer of gibbets, a member of the town council of Edinburgh, the keeper of two mistresses who bore him five children between them. Blood tells. Eventually he was a wanted man for having robbed the Excise Office—not that he needed the money—he was a burglar for the sake of the danger. He died cheerfully on a gibbet of his own devising in seventeen-eighty-eight. *That* is the stuff I am made of!

SANDY. (*A great sigh of relief.*) I might have known you would rise like a phoenix. I am glad I shall not have to worry about you.

BRODIE. Yes, I expect *that* is to be your gift, Sandy— to kill without concern. It is *you* who are dangerous!

SANDY. (*Off-base, very nervous.*) That is not true!

BRODIE. *You* understand nothing of the truth.

SANDY. (*She walks to the door, opens it.*) I think you better *go* now.

BRODIE. (*She just stands, riveted on the spot. Whispers furiously.*) You see yourself as a conqueror, don't you, Sandy? "Kaisarian in all his beauty rare . . ."

SANDY. (*Faintly.*) But you profess to be a great admirer of conquerors, Miss Brodie. (*The* TWO WOMEN *stand, their eyes locked. It is* SANDY *who finally gives way. Her head ducks; her voice barely above a whisper.*) Goodbye, Miss Brodie. (*She shuffles quickly out of the room, out from under the blazing eyes of* MISS BRODIE.)

BRODIE. (*Stares after the* GIRL *for a moment, then walks slowly, almost painfully to the door, stands in its frame for a long beat until a terrible cry comes from her throat and fills the room—and surely finds the ears of* SANDY—*no matter where she has hidden herself.*) AS-SAS-SIIIIIIIINNNNN!

FAST BLACKOUT

ACT THREE

SCENE 8

The Convent Garden again; MR. PERRY *and* HELENA.

MR. PERRY. What do you mean she was "assassinated"? You can't be serious!

HELENA. "Assassinated" was, of course, Miss Brodie's own word. She possessed a colorful vocabulary.

MR. PERRY. But what actually happened to her? Do you know?

HELENA. She was accused of causing a girl's death—called a murderess. She was dismissed from her post.

MR. PERRY. You say she was accused. Was she guilty?

HELENA. Oh—she was very guilty—and very innocent. Depending on which illusion one subscribes to. The illusionist creates his own reality.

MR. PERRY. Creates his own reality? But Sister Helena, such a statement is a direct contradiction to everything you have said to me today.

HELENA. It is?

MR. PERRY. You are the author of a very famous book, every page of which is a polemic *against* illusion.

HELENA. Oh, one should never take a book too seriously. A book—any book—can never be more than the author's opinions—his illusions, if you will—at the moment of writing.

MR. PERRY. But are you saying that you have come to have *different* opinions since writing your book?

HELENA. Since just this moment . . . I had not realized—I simply had not realized—that my book . . . was just one more attempt to get Miss Brodie's attention. Ah —how innocent we *all* are. (*Smiles her final smile of irony, although this time, there is perhaps some humor, too.*) Isn't it all . . . funny?

MR. PERRY. (*A faint pause.*) Perhaps you will not want to answer this question, but I would like to ask if what happened to Miss Brodie was in any way responsible for your decision to enter this convent?

HELENA. Miss Brodie despised what she called "the common moral code." She absolved herself from its . . . strictures. We girls followed her example. As a direct result of this—abandon—I was given a copy of "The City of God." (*A faint smile.*) It was given me by an artist. One of Miss Brodie's most persistent admirers. He gave it to me as a consolation prize. Because I was not lovable.

MR. PERRY. (*Kindly.*) Was this the artist's judgment? Or your own?

HELENA. (*Slowly.*) Oh . . . I think . . . I think it was Miss Brodie's . . .

(*As the lights slowly dim, we hear* MISS BRODIE'S VOICE.)

BRODIE. Little girls, I am in the business of putting old heads on young shoulders and all my pupils are the creme de la creme. Give me a girl at an impressionable age, and she is mine for life . . .

THE END

COSTUME CHART

JEAN BRODIE:
- 2 print dresses
- 1 brown suit (skirt and jacket)
- 1 green tweed coat
- 1 panama-type hat with wide brim and one bunch of nasturtiums on brim
- 1 brown felt hat (cloche style)
- 1 green felt hat
- 1 pair black T-strap shoes
- 1 pair beige T-strap shoes
- 2 pairs nude-colored tights
- 1 print silk blouse
- 1 beige silk blouse

MISS MACKAY:
- 1 pale-yellow windowpane plaid cotton shirt
- 1 white blouse
- 1 lavender silk blouse
- 1 grey wool suit (jacket and skirt)
- 1 black knit suit (jacket and skirt)
- 1 pair black oxfords

MR. LOWTHER:
- 1 green wool kiltie
- 1 green tweed jacket (short with cutaway front)
- 1 grey or tan golf suit—knickers and jacket
- 1 pale-yellow stripe shirt worn with green jacket
- 1 pale-yellow plaid shirt worn with golf suit
- 2 pairs knee high wool socks
- 1 plaid raincoat (tan)
- 1 pair dark brown oxfords
- 1 brown necktie
- 1 sporran (bag) hung around hip; leather or chain strap

GYM TEACHER:
- 1 blue cotton blouse
- 1 black felt or wool skirt
- 1 pair black oxfords
- 1 policeman's whistle

TEDDY LLOYD:
- 1 pair grey trousers
- 1 green corduroy jacket
- 1 raincoat (tan)
- 2 shirts
- 1 pair oxfords
- 1 necktie
- 1 artist's smock

SISTER HELENA:
- 1 tan habit (Poor Clare's order)
- 1 black veil
- 1 rosary beads
- 1 white head piece
- 1 white bib
- 1 pair sandals

MR. PERRY: (reporter)
- 1 conservative dark brown suit
- 1 black and white checked topcoat (carried over arm)
- 1 ecru-colored shirt
- 1 brown necktie
- 1 pair brown slip-on shoes (leather; dressy)

GARDENER:
- 1 pair old trousers
- 1 soiled cotton undershirt
- 1 pair boots (calf-height)
- 1 dingy, old-beaten hat

(TWO) GIRL GUIDES:
- 1 plain dark blue shirt worn over black skirt
- 1 Girl Scout belt
- 1 pair black oxfords
- 1 pair black tights
- 1 black felt four-inch brimmed hat

THE SCHOOLGIRLS:
- (13 schoolgirls including the 4 Brodie girls)
- 13 blue and white striped shirt-style cotton blouses
- 13 Navy-blue jumper-type uniforms:
    - front yoke
    - box pleats
    - self-belt worn below waist

13 pairs black oxfords
13 French blue and Navy striped neckties
13 pairs black tights
13 gym bloomers

SANDY:
1st act uniform as described above
2nd act same uniform but longer length worn with Cuban-heel black suede shoes
1 navy or black felt hat with 2-inch brim; French blue ribbon
1 navy blazer
1 black raincoat: double-breasted with self-belt
1 dressing gown (bathrobe)
1 pair pajamas
1 pair bedroom slippers

MONICA:
1st act uniform as described above
2nd act same uniform but longer length worn with Cuban-heel black suede shoes
1 navy or black felt hat with 2-inch brim; French blue ribbon
1 navy blazer
1 black raincoat: double-breasted with self-belt
1 pair nude tights worn in 2nd act

MARY MACGREGOR:
1st act uniform as described above
2nd act same uniform but longer length worn with Cuban-heel black suede shoes
1 navy or black felt hat with 2-inch brim; French blue ribbon
1 navy blazer
1 black raincoat: double-breasted with self-belt
1 red tartan kiltie skirt
1 very dark green blazer worn with kiltie

JENNIE:
1st act uniform as described above
2nd act same uniform but longer length worn with Cuban-heel black suede shoes
1 navy or black felt hat with 2-inch brim; French blue ribbon
1 navy blazer
1 dull dark print dress worn in artists' scene

FOOTNOTES TO COSTUME CHANGES

1st Classroom Scene:
Binding or tight T shirt, shirt, bloomers, black stockings, black oxfords, gym slip, school tie. Carry on blue book sachel. Handerchief, if needed.

Gallery Scene:
Same costume plus school hat. Carry on: school blazer and guide book (stage left prop table).

Music (Mr. Lowther) *Scene:*
Basic costume, no extras.

1st Locker Room Scene (Traviata, Tango Scene) :
Carry on blazer.

2nd Locker Room Scene (Torture Scene) :
Wear school hat. Carry on book bag and raincoat.

Picnic Scene:
Just basic costume.

1st Studio Scene:
Wear school sweater.

 Carry on:
 Raincoat, straw hat, 3 paintings.

 Carry off:
 Just raincoat.

Gym Scene:
Remove gym slip, tie, black oxfords, wear sneakers.

Cross-Over:
Basic costume.

Act Two Costume:
Beige tights, heeled shoes, gym slip, tie, sweater, shirt. Also, anything to show new bosom development (i.e. remove binding). Nothing to carry on.

PROP LIST

ACT ONE

Scene 1:
Convent bench with backing
Zip case (Mr. Perry) with book: "The Transfiguration of the Commonplace"

Scene 2:
School notebooks
10 well worn and inked history primers
10 pencil boxes
30 pencils for girls
10 school notebooks in Brodie's desk
Portrait of Stanley Baldwin on the blackboard (remains there throughout show)
2 reproductions of a Secular Giotto to be hung on the blackboard during the action
Blackboard chalk
Blackboard eraser
5 museum catalogues
2 low stools (off R. S.)

Scene 6:
Practical, period portable gramophone
2 records for the gramophone
Large drawing pad (Sandy)
Paper bag of sweets (practical—Mary)
2 field hockey sticks
1 set of knee pads
6 book satchels (Mary's should be the most expensive looking)
Book on bench R. S. (Mary)

Scene 7:
Giotto postcard with the following text:
"The incomparable Giotto frescoes. How triumphantly his figures vibrate with life, casting off the formalities of decadent Byzantium." Yours truly, J. Brodie

Scene 8:
Bag of sweets ("Rosebuds"—practical—Jenny)
Keys on key ring (Mackay)

Scene 9:

  Mackay's seat
  Stool
  Arrangement of chrysanthemums for Mackay's desk (off L.)
  Practical English and Latin dictionaries for desk
  Register, diary, pen, ink and blotter on the desk

Scene 10:

  Wheelbarrow filled with freshly mown **grass**
  Potted plants arrangement on the S. R. steps (for the green-
    house)
  Parasol (Brodie)
  1 very large straw coloured picnic hamper containing:
    6 cups
    6 plates
    6 napkins
    Plate for the practical sandwiches
    Plate for the practical cake
    Plate for the practical white bread
    Plate for the practical bananas
    Large thermos with tea
    Small thermos with milk
  1 large tartan blanket
  Practical mandolin (Lowther)

ACT TWO

Scene 2:

  3 awkward bundles of groceries (Lowther)
  1 umbrella—black (Brodie)
  1 black umbrella (Sandy)

Scene 3:

  Easel with canvas (portrait of Jenny)
  Painting brushes, palette, rags and canvas cover
  Large, old period radio
  Stack of 4 paintings (various sizes but none any larger than
    20″ x 24″)
  Finished painting of a boy nude (seen by audience—
    20″ x 24″)
  1 draping material for Jenny
  3 throws (dressing)
  2 bolsters
  Painting of Lloyd's family (8 people seen by audience—
    20″ x 24″)

Scene 4:
  Gym dressing (set)
  Practical whistle (Campbell)
  Golf bag with clubs (new, child's set—Sandy)
  Golf bag with clubs (Very old—Brodie)

Scene 5:
  Very old piece of paper (15″ x 11″ approximately) with the
    text from pp. 54-55.

Scene 6:
  Large photograph of Dante meeting Beatrice to fasten to
    blackboard

ACT THREE

Scene 2:
  Practical book of Freudian psychology (Sandy)
  Pile of papers with a large, thick copy of St. Augustine's
    "The City of God" on top (practical)
  Another painting on the easel (of Sandy)
  1 cheap tray
  1 bottle half full of milk (practical)
  Tea pot (practical)
  2 tin mugs (practical)
  Small stool (off L.)

Scene 4:
  Large map of Spain covering the whole blackboard
  Marking pencil for the map
  Small notebook (Lloyd)
  Fountain pen, period (Lloyd)
  Newspaper (Brodie) off L.

Scene 5:
  4 text books (in Brodie desk)

Scene 6:
  No props

Scene 7:
  Padded covering with fringe for the Brodie desk at the low
    trim (ottoman for Sandy)
  Book:—"St. Augustine" (Sandy)
  Handbag (Brodie)

Other Publications for Your Interest

TALKING WITH . . .
(LITTLE THEATRE)
By JANE MARTIN

11 women—Bare stage

Here, at last, is the collection of eleven extraordinary monologues for eleven actresses which had them on their feet cheering at the famed Actors Theatre of Louisville—audiences, critics and, yes, even jaded theatre professionals. The mysteriously pseudonymous Jane Martin is truly a "find", a new writer with a wonderfully idiosyncratic style, whose characters alternately amuse, move and frighten us always, however, speaking to use from the depths of their souls. The characters include a baton twirler who has found God through twirling; a fundamentalist snake handler, an ex-rodeo rider crowded out of the life she has cherished by men in 3-piece suits who want her to dress up "like Minnie damn Mouse in a tutu"; an actress willing to go to any length to get a job; and an old woman who claims she once saw a man with "cerebral walrus" walk into a McDonald's and be healed by a Big Mac. "Eleven female monologues, of which half a dozen verge on brilliance."—London Guardian. "Whoever (Jane Martin) is, she's a writer with an original imagination."—Village Voice. "With Jane Martin, the monologue has taken on a new poetic form, intensive in its method and revelatory in its impact."—Philadelphia Inquirer. "A dramatist with an original voice . . . (these are) tales about enthusiasms that become obsessions, eccentric confessionals that levitate with religious symbolism and gladsome humor."—N.Y. Times. *Talking With . . .* is the 1982 winner of the American Theatre Critics Association Award for Best Regional Play.　　　　　　　　　　　　　　　　(#22009)

HAROLD AND MAUDE
(ADVANCED GROUPS—COMEDY)
By COLIN HIGGINS

9 men, 8 women—Various settings

Yes: *the Harold and Maude!* This is a stage adaptation of the wonderful movie about the suicidal 19-year-old boy who finally learns how to truly *live* when he meets up with that delightfully whacky octogenarian, Maude. Harold is the proverbial Poor Little Rich Kid. His alienation has caused him to attempt suicide several times, though these attempts are more cries for attention than actual attempts. His peculiar attachment to Maude, whom he meets at a funeral (a mutual passion), is what saves him—and what captivates us. This new stage version, a hit in France directed by the internationally-renowned Jean-Louis Barrault, will certainly delight both afficionados of the film and new-comers to the story. "Offbeat upbeat comedy."—Christian Science Monitor.　　　　　　　(#10032)

Other Publications for Your Interest

AGNES OF GOD
(LITTLE THEATRE—DRAMA)

By JOHN PIELMEIER

3 women—1 set (bare stage)

Doctor Martha Livingstone, a court-appointed psychiatrist, is asked to determine the sanity of a young nun accused of murdering her own baby. Mother Miriam Ruth, the nun's superior, seems bent on protecting Sister Agnes from the doctor, and Livingstone's suspicions are immediately aroused. In searching for solutions to various mysteries (who killed the baby? Who fathered the child?) Livingstone forces all three women, herself included, to face some harsh realities in their own lives, and to re-examine the meaning of faith and the commitment of love. "Riveting, powerful, electrifying new drama . . . three of the most magnificent performances you will see this year on any stage anywhere . . . the dialogue crackles."—Rex Reed, N.Y. Daily News. ". . . outstanding play . . . deals intelligently with questions of religion and psychology."—Mel Gussow, N.Y. Times. ". . . unquestionably blindingly theatrical . . . cleverly executed blood and guts evening in the theatre . . . three sensationally powered performances calculated to wring your withers."—Clive Barnes, N.Y. Post.   (#236)

COME BACK TO THE 5 & DIME, JIMMY DEAN, JIMMY DEAN
(ADVANCED GROUPS—DRAMA)

By ED GRACZYK

1 man, 8 women—Interior

In a small-town dime store in West Texas, the Disciples of James Dean gather for their twentieth reunion. Now a gaggle of middle-aged women, the Disciples were teenagers when Dean filmed "Giant" two decades ago in nearby Marfa. One of them, an extra in the film, has a child whom she says was conceived by Dean on the "Giant" set; the child is the Jimmy Dean of the title. The ladies' reminiscences mingle with flash-backs to their youth; then the arrival of a stunning and momentarily unrecognized woman sets off a series of confrontations that upset their self-deceptions and expose their well-hidden disappointments. "Full of homespun humor . . . surefire comic gems."—N.Y. Post. "Captures convincingly the atmosphere of the 1950s."—Women's Wear Daily.   (#5147)